# BILLABØNG

## RADITYA RONDI

Golden sunset glass-off at Lance's Right, aka HT's. Photographer: Pete Frieden

# DISCOVER
# THE WORLD'S BEST RIGHTS

HT'S, MENTAWAI ISLANDS

EXPLORE
THE WORLD'S BEST LEFTS

DESERT POINT, LOMBOK

EXPERIENCE
THE WORLD'S BEST TUBES

LAGUNDRI, NIAS

ENJOY THE LONGEST
RIDES OF YOUR LIFE

IMPOSSIBLES, BALI

D

# SURF INTO THE SUNSET
# IN THE LAND OF LEFTS

IMPOSSIBLES, BALI

E

Time it right, and you might get an hour alone. Photo: Mick Curley

# ESCAPE THE CROWDS
# EVEN IN BALI?

BALANGAN, BALI

F

Asu, Hinako Islands, Sumatra. Before The Earthquake. Now even hollower. Photo: JS Callahan/ tropicalpix

BEST SEAT IN THE HOUSE

G

Grajagan. Photo: Alan Van Gysen

# EXPLORE WHERE THE REEF MEETS THE JUNGLE

G-LAND, EAST JAVA

# WANT TO PUT YOURSELF IN THIS PICTURE?

Photo: Tim McKenna

The view from your room at Surf Camp Sumatra: www.surfcampsumatra.com

MENTAWAI DREAMING

SUMATRA DREAMING

Is this "The Longest, Best Tube in the World"? Desert Point, Lombok. Photo: Jon Huberman

Is this "The Longest, Shallowest, Deadliest Tube in the World"? One Palm Point, West Java. Photo: Tipi Jabrik

# YOU WANT LONG TUBES?

DESERT POINT. LOMBOK

## GET ONBOARD
## WAKE UP TO THIS EVERY DAY

ONE PALM POINT, PANAITAN ISLAND

# ANY SECRET SPOTS STILL?

Sorry, can't say where. Photo: Jon Huberman

Felipe Pomar, "remote spice island". Photo: Per Ranheimer

GO FOR A PADDLE
SEE WHAT YOU MIGHT FIND

Uninhabited. Yacht access only. Photo: Stuart Horstman, Freeline Indonesian Surf Adventures - www.freelinesurf.com.au

# SECRET SPOT #9,999?

# 20 YEARS OF DISCOVERY

In the 20 years since **Indo Surf & Lingo** was first published, there have been many exciting new surf discoveries in Indonesia. Feedback we've received shows this book has helped inspire quite a few adventurous souls to venture where no surfer has gone before. Surfers are one of the few lucky "tribes" on the planet still able to enjoy the rewards of exploration.

While Bali is still the best starting point for your first trip, if you speak a little Indonesian, the outer islands can deliver incredible rewards for the truly adventurous among us. But even if you don't get out of the comfort of Kuta Beach, try to learn some "**Indo lingo**". It will make a huge positive difference to your trip.

The first surfers to discover the perfection of Sumatra's **Mentawai Islands** all learnt enough basic Indonesian to enlist the help of local fishermen who knew these treacherous waters better than anyone (up till then). These days Padang harbour in Sumatra has become a major base for over 30 yachts venturing out to the Mentawais and beyond. This book actually started out as a language guidebook, because it's still the best way to escape the crowds and discovery your own perfect surfing paradise.

Java, Lombok, Sumbawa, Sumba, Timor and many of the 17,000 other remote "**Spice Islands**" still have unexplored areas slowly revealing their hidden treasures each year to surfers who dare to roam off the beaten track. Secrets are still out there.

As you travel through Indonesia, enjoying your holiday of a lifetime, please remember how lucky we all are to be "free-and-easy surfers", born now into this age of cheap air travel.

In all the history of mankind, there will only be **One Generation** that will be **The First** to explore the world through the eyes of The Travelling Surfer. We are part of this lucky generation. As children we could only dream of undiscovered Tropical Waves. Yet by the time of our old age these dreams can become reality, familiar "second homes" to us, joyful new playgrounds in the short history of surf exploration. How lucky we are.

One hundred years ago mankind could only travel by sailing ship. To travel to "The Far East" would take years. These days it's just a day away in an air-conditioned airplane.

One hundred years from now, air travel in oil-powered jets will almost certainly no longer be possible. Surfing in a clean, un-polluted ocean may also become impossible if **Our Generation** does not spread positive ideas and inspiration while we enjoy this unique luxury of international air travel.

Go far but tread lightly. Search and discover, but also continue to learn and educate. Spread your knowledge and insights so that future generations can continue to share this stoke that only a surfer knows. Let your journey begin...

Surfing on the Razor's edge - The Search is endless. Photo: Mark Newsham courtesy Rip Curl.

# SEARCH & DISCOVER
## respect & protect

"Twenty years from now you will be more disappointed by the things that you didn't do than by the ones you did do. So throw off the bowlines. Sail away from the safe harbor. Catch the trade winds in your sails. Explore. Dream. Discover." Mark Twain

Photo : JS Callahan / tropicalpix

**RIP CURL**

# NEW DISCOVERIES

New Discovery, not yet surfed because nearby waves are better and less deadly. "Melon Busters" Photo by Jon Huberman
Photos opposite from top left to right: Lakey Pipe - thanks to Indo Jiwa. Hideaways by daniah. Nokandui - daniah. HT's - daniah.
HT's tuberide - by daniah. The S Spot - John Hepler. Desert Point - Mark Newsham. Hideaways - Ethan Ford, Wave Park Resort.

For the last 20 years this guidebook has helped thousands of surfers explore the magical islands of Bali, Java, Sumatra, Mentawais, Lombok, Sumbawa, Sumba, Timor, Rote and the 17,000 other uniquely special Indonesian "Spice Islands".

- The **Indo Surf** pages will help you find uncrowded surf in all Indonesian islands, even in Bali.
- The **Trip Planner** pages will help you decide where to go, to catch the waves you want, and make the most of your holiday.
- The **Indo Language** pages will help you learn to speak Indonesian quickly and easily, so you can more easily explore the exotic Indonesian outer islands, in search of your own secret spots, for **The Adventure of a Lifetime**.

More than ever, after the tragic 2002 and 2005 "Bali bombs", being able to speak even a little of the Indonesian language will make a huge difference to your trip. You won't be regarded as "just another tourist", but rather seen as a "respectful traveller". It will open up wonderful experiences for you with the friendly Indonesian people, offering insights into their uniquely spiritual lives.
As **Tracks** magazine wrote about this book: "There's nothing better than being able to communicate in a foreign country. It will earn you respect with the locals and get you closer to the culture - and the tube!"

This book delivers to you all the knowledge of Indonesian surfing and language gained by the author over the last 35 years, plus essential courtesies, cultural hints and travel tips that will hopefully save you lots of time, stress and money.
We hope this book helps you enjoy a life-enhancing experience in Indonesia that you will treasure forever.

# LEARN TO SPEAK INDONESIAN
## and you could discover new indo surf spots like these!

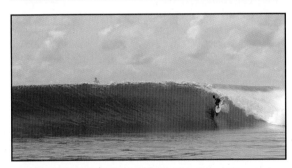

The surfing world first heard about Bali in the early 1970's. **Kuta Reef** was the first major discovery, soon followed by **Uluwatu** in 1971 and **Padang**. Then surfers started exploring other islands and discovered two of the world's best waves: **Grajagan** "the ultimate left" in 1972, and **Nias**, "the perfect right" in 1975. New discoveries in the **Mentawai Islands** are even better.

Most of the surf breaks in this book are relatively well known within the worldwide surfing community. But there are many other "**Secret Spots**" and new discoveries which we have respected by keeping secret. These spots await you.

The key to exploring for uncrowded waves in Indonesia is to study the language lessons in this book, and enlist the help of the friendly Indonesian local surfers. And then to respect their secret spots by keeping them a secret.

# TRIP PLANNER

## FIRST TRIP TO INDO ?

If it's your first trip to Indonesia, or even your first trip overseas, **BALI** is best for a great variety of things to see and do, with a level of comfort and ease that can be harder to find in other islands. Bali has been voted "**Worlds Best Holiday Island**" for decades, from backpackers to luxury travel enthusiasts.

Bali offers you great hotels on any budget, from $10 to $1,000 a night, good food from $1 a meal to $25, easy transport to the surf, exciting cultural sightseeing, adventure sports, and cheap shopping for when the surf is flat. Bali has it all made easy!

If your total budget is closer to **$50 a day** than $1,000, then Indonesia is ideal for you. "Losmen" home-stay hotels have private rooms from $10 to $25 a night. "Warung" meals cost from $1 to $10. Transport is cheap with motorbike rentals from $10 a day. You can even get by on total $30 a day, although **$50** is more comfortable. Most surf beaches in Bali have losmen close by from $10 to $25. So Bali gets the vote for first trip!

See Page 106 for our recommended **Hotel** and **Surf Camp** options all over the Indonesian islands for every budget level.

## 2nd TRIP TO INDO

You've been to Bali, loved it, but are ready for the next adventure. Assuming surf is your first priority, then go to **Bali** again but add a 10 day yacht trip. **Dreamweaver**, **Moggy** and **Partama** leave Bali for the islands of **Nusa Lembongan, Lombok** and **Sumbawa**, surfing a range of great waves from fun Playgrounds to hollow Desert Point, often claimed "Best Wave in the World".

## 10th TRIP TO INDO

You already know and love Indo, but are looking for more unique experiences off the beaten track. If you're a competent surfer and have already done the essentials of **G-LAND** and the **MENTAWAIS**, then maybe explore east to **Timor** and island hop from **Rote** to **Sumba**. Or check north of **Nias**. Or try the **Sumatra** mainland. Or even go exploring for "off-season" waves in Indonesia's Pacific from **Halmahera** to **Morotai**. Get a **60 day visa** in advance for these longer trips, and be prepared for a lot more than just another surf adventure. Get out there!

## BEST HONEYMOON & FAMILY

Once again **BALI** is best. Comfort and a bit of luxury at great value prices. Beachfront 4-star resorts are about $100 a double. For surfers we can recommend **Discovery Kartika Plaza** and **Poppies Cottages** Kuta; **Blue Point Villas & Spa** Uluwatu; **Puri Raja Hotel** Legian; **Puri Dana Villa** Seminyak; **Lembongan Beach Villas** Nusa Lembongan; and in the Mentawai islands **Togat Nusa, Kandui Villas, Aloita** and **Wave Park** resorts.

## LEAST CROWDED ?

Finding a groovy beach villa with perfect uncrowded waves out front is getting rarer these days, and isn't cheap, but these Mentawai resorts guarantee it: **Wave Park, Kandui, Togat, Aloita** or new **Aura**; Also 5-star **Nihiwatu** in Sumba.

## YOUR SURF ABILITY?

A major thing to consider is your surfing ability. What kind of waves do you **really** want to experience in Indonesia? Relaxing beachbreaks or life-threatening tube rides? Of course if the swell hits 10 feet everywhere will be challenging, but the breaks listed below are less hollow and dangerous **most** of the time:

## LEARNING TO SURF

**Kuta** and **Legian** in Bali are best for first time beginners. Five kilometres of sandy beachbreaks, with surfboard rentals, hotels and surf schools on the beach. The most professional surf schools are **Rip Curl School of Surf** in Legian and **Pro Surf** in Kuta. Most other surf breaks in Indonesia are far too dangerous for learning, breaking over sharp coral reefs, except for Bali's **Dreamland Beach**, and **Batu Karas** in West Java.

The new **Kima Surf Camps** are very popular with learners and intermediate surfers who want to experience the surfing lifestyle for a week or two, sharing surf trips and evenings with fellow surfing enthusiasts. **Kima Surf** has four camps in Bali for all levels of experience - www.kimasurf.com, Ph: 0361 736 737

## INTERMEDIATE

You're becoming a relatively competent surfer, or maybe don't surf as often as you used to, aren't in peak fitness, or would prefer to enjoy more relaxed cruisy sessions in the water. OK, these are the breaks for you, up to around head high or 6 feet:

**Bali**. See F.A.Q. page 119 for Bali's easier breaks. Or let **Bali Surfing Tours** show you all the spots: www.bali-surfing.com. **Lombok**. Grupuk, Mawi and Ekas are great fun reef breaks. **Nusa Lembongan**. Playgrounds is just 2 hours from Bali. **Batu Karas, West Java**. Gentle sandy point, fun for longboards or the less advanced. www.javacovebeachhotel.com **Cimaja, West Java**. Nice right hand point, not too hollow. Stay 5 minutes walk away at **Pondok Kencana Resort**. **Tarimbang, Sumba**. A super fun long righthander **Nemberala, Roti**. Long left reef break. "A softer G-Land" **Sumbawa**. Nungas is a slower left. Lakey Peak a fun tube **Krui Sumatra**. Sumatra's Longest Left. www.freeline.com.au

## ADVANCED

You're keen to push yourself into bigger waves, hollower tubes. Time to score the best waves of your life! Here's our pick: **Mentawais**. Awesome variety of "The World's Best" waves. On a 10 day yacht trip you'll see dozens of breaks, and probably catch the most memorable rides of your life. #1 pick for sure! Head for Kandui, HT's, Telescopes, Bankvaults - it's all good! **Panaitan Island**. Hollowest lefts and rights on the planet. **G-Land**. Goofy heaven. Consistently overhead all year. **Lombok**. Desert Point. Longest fastest tubes on Earth! **Nias**. Nirvana for natural footers. 9 second tubes possible. **Sumba**. Nihiwatu is Indo's least crowded world-class left **Bali**. Padang-Padang is the double barrelled Indo Pipeline. **Anywhere, anytime**. Every break can be world-class on its day! With a 10 foot swell, even the beachbreak at Halfway Kuta will give you tube rides to remember. Pull in and don't look back!

# THE BEST SURF CAMPS, YACHTS & TRAVEL AGENTS

## ALL INDONESIA
**FREELINE Indo Surf Adventures** - www.freelinesurf.com.au
Freecall Stuart in Sydney: 1800 280 626, +61 2 4268 4621

**THE PERFECT WAVE** - ALL Indo www.theperfectwave.com.au
Ph Jamie in Sydney: 1300 009 283, +61 2 9939 0890

**KIMA SURFARIS** - ALL Indo - www.kimasurf.com
**NOMAD SURFERS** - ALL Indo - www.nomadsurfers.com

## BALI
**KIMA SURF CAMPS** – www.kimasurf.com - Ph 736 737
**KERAMAS SURF LODGE** - East Bali - www.nomadsurfers.com
**WORLD SURFARIS** - www.worldsurfaris.com 1800 611 163

## BALI- LEMBONGAN- LOMBOK-
**DREAMWEAVER** - www.dreamweaver-surf.com 0813 38355228
**MOGGY Charters** - www.moggybali.com +62 81 139 8434
**KIMA SURFARIS** – www.kimasurf.com +62 361 736 737
**WORLD SURFARIS** - www.worldsurfaris.com, 1800 611 163
**SRI NOA NOA** Yacht Charters - www.cruisebali.com

## G-LAND
**G-Land JOYO'S JUNGLE Surf Camp** - www.g-land.com
**WORLD SURFARIS** - www.worldsurfaris.com 1800 611 163

## WEST JAVA
**BATU BESAR Losmen**, Turtles - www.freelinesurf.com.au
**JAVA COVE**, Batu Karas - www.javacovebeachhotel.com

## PANAITAN ISLAND
**JUST DREAMING** - www.freelinesurf.com.au

## MENTAWAI ISLANDS
**SUMATRAN SURFARIS** - www.sumatransurfariis.com
Ph Scuzz: Sumatra +62 0812 667 2899 - USA: 415 297 4837
**SARAINA KOAT MENTAWAI** - www.mentawaiislands.co.id
Ph or SMS Jordan or Rudi in Mentawais: +62 812 66 40941
**KANDUI VILLAS** - www.kanduivillas.com +62 812 66 40941

**ARIMBI Mentawai Surf Charters** - www.surftravel.com.au
**SURGING WATERS** - Kaimana - www.surgingwaters.com
**TOGAT NUSA RETREAT** - www.togatnusaretreat.com
**ALOITA RESORT & SPA** - www.aloitaresort.com 62 759 320354
**MENTAWAI BLUE** - NagaLaut - www.mentawaiblue.com
**THE PERFECT WAVE** - www.theperfectwave.com.au
**FREELINE Indo Surf Adventures** - www.freelinesurf.com.au

## SUMATRAN MAINLAND
**OMBAK INDAH** Losmen, Krui - www.freelinesurf.com.au
**AURA Surf Resort**, North Sumatra - www.aurasurfresort.com

## SUMBA & ROTE
**NEMBERALA** - Malole www.rotesurfhouse.com 081337 767412
**Mr DAVID'S** - www.eastsumba.com $35 Fax: +62 387 61333

## BALI SURF SCHOOLS
**SUP BALI**, Lessons, SUP Sales & Rentals www.supbali.com
**PRO SURF** Halfway Kuta - www.prosurfschool.com 744 1466

## ALL INDONESIA
**WORLD SURFARIS** - ALL Indo - www.worldsurfaris.com
Freecall Shaun in Aust: 1800 611 163, +61 7 5444 4011

**SUrF TRaVeL ONLiNe** - ALL Indo - www.surftravelonline.com
Ph Pete, Kuta: + 62 361 737 056, Mobile: +62 818 348 824

**SURF TRAVEL COMPANY** - ALL Indo www.surftravel.com.au
**THE INDO ODYSSEY** - ALL Indo - www. indo-odyssey.com

**BALI SURFING TOURS** - www.bali-surfing.com 081933102420
**PURI DANA VILLA** - 5-Star Seminyak: www.puridana.com
**THE PERFECT WAVE** - www.theperfectwave.com.au

## SUMBAWA
**NOMAD Tropical Resort** Sumbawa www.nomadsurfers.com
**LEMBONGAN BEACH VILLAS** - www.lembonganbeachvillas.com
**AMAN GATI HOTEL, Lakey** - www.surftravelonline.com
**THE PERFECT WAVE** - www.theperfectwave.com.au

**BOBBY'S G-LAND Surf Resort** - www.grajagan.com
**THE PERFECT WAVE** - www.theperfectwave.com.au

**PONDOK KENCANA Resort**, Cimaja - www.ombaktujuh.net
**FREELINE Indo Surf Adventures** - www.freelinesurf.com.au

**JUST DREAMING** – www.justdreamingsurfsafaris.com

**NUSA DEWATA** Surf Charters - www.nusadewata.com
Ph Simon and Siti in Padang: +62 811 661 4483

**NUSANTARA** Surf Charters - www.thenusantara.com
**PELURU** Mentawai Speedboat - www.indosurfboat.com

**ADDICTION** Luxury Catamaran - www.addictionsurfing.com
**WAVE PARK RESORT** - www.wavepark.com +628126635551
**AURA SURF RESORT** - www.aurasurfresort.com 62759 320388
**KIMA SURF** – www.kimasurf.com +62 361 736 737
**WORLD SURFARIS** - www.worldsurfaris.com 1800 611 163
**SUrF TRaVeL ONLiNe** - www.surftravelonline.com 737 056
**NOMAD SURFERS** - www.nomadsurfers.com
**QUEST 1 NEPTUNE** - www.theneptuneadventures.com

## NIAS, ASU + TELO ISLANDS
**Puri Asu VIP Villa**, Asu Hinako islands - www.vipasu.com
**Boraspati Nias Tours**, Medan. Tom: www.boraspati.com
**Telo Islands Lattitude Zero** - www.worldsurfaris.com

**SRI NOA NOA** Yacht Charters - www.cruisebali.com
**TARIMBANG** - www.surftravelonline.com. Ph Bali 737 056

**RIP CURL School of Surf**, "Blue Ocean" Legian. Ph 73 58 58
**BALI KITE SURF** - www.bali-kitesurfing.org Sanur: 284 260

# INDO SURF SEASONS
## when should I go?

**Bali** offers over 30 top-quality waves on the west and east coasts of the island, which are just **half an hour** apart by car or motorbike. You'll find offshore winds virtually every day all year.

**The Dry** winter season is offshore on the famous Kuta to Uluwatu west coast, with south-east trade winds from early **April** to late **October**. This is the best season for quality surf and guaranteed sunshine, the best time to plan your first trip.

**The Wet** summer season is offshore on the Nusa Dua to Keramas east side of the island, with north-west winds usually from **January** to late **March**. This is the least crowded season. Although rain averages 2 inches a day in January and February, there can still be a week of sunny weather with perfect surf.

Between seasons can be less predictable, but you can usually find offshore waves somewhere. The biggest swells usually arrive mid-winter from May to September, although tropical cyclones during summer can send up a few days of solid swell.

Most surfers prefer the consistent sunny winter months with the largest swell activity, rather than the humid monsoon months when rain squalls can be more frequent than world-class surf. Unfortunately this means that between June and August every year you will usually have to share Uluwatu with 100 other hot surfers from Brazil, Hawaii, Australia, America, South Africa, Europe and Japan... and the local Balinese surfers rip too!

Luckily though, Indonesia's outer islands offer lots of less crowded waves during these months, from South Sumatra down through Java, Lombok, Sumbawa, Sumba, the West Timor islands, and even Irian Jaya. It is with this in mind that this guidebook has been created, especially to help the adventurous surfer-traveller exploring the more remote Outer Islands.

The major exception is **the Mentawais** which enjoy far more glassy days due to Equatorial doldrums. Plus yachts can quickly motor around the small islands to find wind-protected reefs. Conditions can be perfect **all year**, with average 4-8 feet from May to October, and fun 3-5 feet the rest of the year.

**How to Avoid Crowds in Bali**. Not easy anymore, but first read all the info describing each break in Bali. Then go to page 46 **"Where Will We Surf Today?"** for three pages that chart your alternatives on any wind direction, tide or swell size. Sometimes most of the crowd automatically goes to the biggest and best spot for that day's conditions. But you can use this guide to slip away to another spot that while maybe not quite as big or perfect, still has excellent waves with less crowds. Or try the other side at dawn hoping for an hour or three of glass.

One tip to remember is that most Bali waves get better in the afternoons, after the trade wind has straightened the swell out, so sometimes the early mornings aren't too crowded. The sun comes up around 6:30 am. The surf doesn't get too crowded until 9 am after most tourists finish their buffet breakfast.

Photo: Sebastian Imizcoz, Saraina Koat Mentawai

Lovina Photo: Sebastian Imizcoz, Saraina Koat Mentawai

www.mentawaiislands.co.id

Photo: Sebastian Imizcoz, Saraina Koat Mentawai

# BALI SURF SPOTS

## DRY SEASON  20-37
## west coast - may to september

| | |
|---|---|
| Uluwatu | 22 |
| Padang-Padang | 26 |
| Impossibles | 29 |
| Bingin | 28 |
| Dreamland | 30 |
| Balangan | 30 |
| Jimbaran | 31 |
| Airport Rights | 31 |
| Airport Lefts | 31 |
| Kuta Reef | 32 |
| Kuta Beach | 33 |
| Halfway | 33 |
| Legian | 34 |
| Canggu | 36 |
| Pererenan | 36 |
| Balian | 37 |
| Medewi | 37 |
| Nusa Lembongan | 45 |

## WET SEASON  38-44
## east coast - december to march

| | |
|---|---|
| Nusa Dua | 39 |
| Sri Lanka | 40 |
| Turtle Island | 40 |
| Hyatt Reef | 41 |
| Tanjung Sari | 41 |
| Sanur | 42 |
| Padang Galak | 43 |
| Keramas | 43 |
| Lebih | 43 |
| Padang Bai | 43 |
| Nyang Nyang | 38 |
| Green Ball | 38 |

# INDONESIA
## SURFING TREASURE MAP

ACEH

SUMATRA

NIAS

MENTAWAI ISLANDS

PADANG

SINGAPORE

BRUNEI

KALIMANTAN

KRAKATAU

JAKARTA

JAVA

BALI SUMBAWA

LOMBOK

SUMB

MB

Ferry to Java

GILIMANUK

NEGARA

SINGARAJA

GUNUNG BATUR

GUNUNG AGUNG

# BALI

0  6  12  18  24 KM

N

Ferry to Lomb

## BALI SURF SPOTS

1. Uluwatu
2. Padang
3. Bingin
4. Balangan
5. Jimbaran
6. Airport Rights
7. Airport Lefts
8. Kuta Reef
9. Kuta Beach
10. Legian Beach
11. Oberoi
12. Canggu
13. Balian
14. Medewi

15. Nyang Nyang
16. Green Ball
17. Nusa Dua
18. Sri Lanka
19. Turtle Island
20. Hyatt Reef
21. Tanjung Sari
22. Sanur
23. Padang Galak
24. Keramas
25. Lebih
26. Padang Bai
27. Lembongan

DENPASAR

SANUR

NUSA LEMBONGAN

NUSA PENIDA

KUTA

NUSA DUA

ULUWATU

© indo surf & lingo

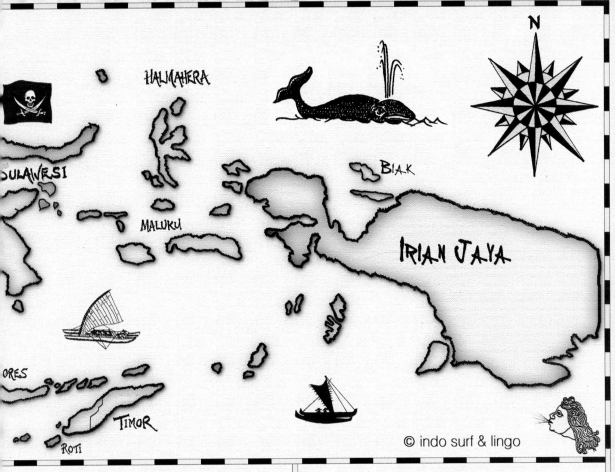

HALMAHERA

SULAWESI

MALUKU

BIAK

IRIAN JAYA

ORES

TIMOR

ROTI

© indo surf & lingo

## ULUWATU TO CANGGU

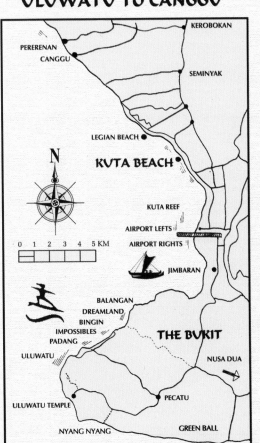

KEROBOKAN

PERERENAN
CANGGU

SEMINYAK

N

LEGIAN BEACH

KUTA BEACH

KUTA REEF

AIRPORT LEFTS

AIRPORT RIGHTS

0 1 2 3 4 5 KM

JIMBARAN

BALANGAN
DREAMLAND
BINGIN
IMPOSSIBLES
PADANG

THE BUKIT

ULUWATU

NUSA DUA

ULUWATU TEMPLE

PECATU

NYANG NYANG

GREEN BALL

## KUTA AND LEGIAN

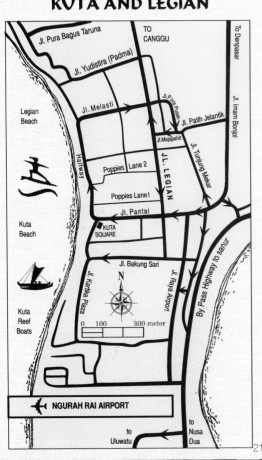

Jl. Pura Bagus Taruna

TO CANGGU

To Denpasar

Jl. Yudistira (Padma)

Legian Beach

Jl. Melasti

Jl. Pura Puseh

Jl. Patih Jelantik

Jl. Imam Bonjol

Jl. Majapahit

Halfway

Poppies Lane 2

JL. LEGIAN

Jl. Tunjung Mekar

Poppies Lane1

Kuta Beach

Jl. Pantai

KUTA SQUARE

By Pass Highway to sanur

Jl. Bakung Sari

N

Kuta Reef Boats

Jl. Kartika Plaza

Jl. Raya Airport

0    100      300 meter

✈ NGURAH RAI AIRPORT

to Uluwatu

to Nusa Dua

# BALI WEST COAST
# dry season - april to october

## 01. ULUWATU

The first time you see the famous lineup of Uluwatu will be a sight you will remember forever. Imagine what it was like for young Steve Cooney and Rusty Miller when they first paddled out through the cave in 1971, surfing over coral without legropes!

Uluwatu is Bali's most consistent left. Almost always 4 foot plus, so almost always crowded too. But you can score less crowded early sessions by staying at one of the new bungalows nearby. Hang all day on the clifftop enjoying cheap food, drinks, great views of the surf, and relaxing après-surf massages.

At **high tide** you surf the section known as **The Peak**, straight out from **The Cave**, with classic tubes right from the jacking take-off. Unfortunately one in three tubes tends to close down unpredictably, so be prepared to duck out through the back.

**Low tide** causes **The Peak** to close out, so you surf 100 metres further down the reef at **The Racetrack.** A series of long walled sections link together with predictable open tubes that lure you into the next curving bowl - but don't go too far, because like most Indo reef breaks, it eventually closes out savagely onto almost dry coral that is very sharp - wear **reef boots** at all tides!

Over 10 feet at low tide, Racetrack breaks further out at **Outside Corner**, a thick pushy wall that rolls evenly for 100 to 200 metres. There are rarely tubes, but the faces are ideal for big carving manoeuvres. A great place to push yourself into tackling bigger surf. On high tide the **Bombie** looms up way out the back.

**Temples** is the line-up furthest south, almost out of sight. A good outside reef to avoid the crowds or find more juice on smaller days. To save a few hundred metres of paddling, walk along the beach as far south as possible before paddling out.

### First time tip
You need to come back in through The Cave, but the current is always fast, so aim for the beach 50 metres up-current. On big days, it's sometimes safer to get out of the water by drifting down to Padang, 2Km north.

Typical small day at Uluwatu showing high tide Peak, clifftop Warungs and Blue Point Villas. Photo Nathan Lawrence

The Peak

Outside Corner, Made Lana

Made Lana, Photo Jon Huberman

Temples

Bombie

Peak

Outside Corner

Racetrack

Uluwatu. Photo: JS Callahan / tropicalpix

23

Outside Corner. Sean Woolnough

As big as it gets.May 2007.   Photo Kadek Uluwatuphoto

Racetrack

Uluwatu Cave Photo Emiliano Cataldi

The Peak

Outside Corner

# 02 PADANG-PADANG

Pronounced "**Pah-dung**". Real name Labuhan Sait. Bali's hollowest, most dangerous left, tubing over very shallow coral. Only breaks on big swells when Uluwatu is getting out-of-control, over 10 or 12 feet. The only way to make the wave is to backdoor the 2nd tube section in front of the cliff, so it is a place for experts only, safest at high tide. Low tide gets insane but deadly.

To get there, turn off the Uluwatu road at Pecatu village. Padang is a great place to watch the best surfers in the world tackling one of the most awesome tubes on the planet. You can sit comfortably in warungs on the beach and count the number of broken boards! Unfortunately, it is very dangerous under 5 feet because it breaks so close to the cliff. Definitely not for learners.

Mustofa Jeksen, Photo:JEP John Hepler

Padang. Photo: JS Callahan / tropicalpix

It's too easy to get shipwrecked at Padang. Photo Nathan Lawrence

Rahtu, "Mr Bali" Gusti Somer's son, a 2nd generation Bali surfer.  Photo courtesy Billabong

## 03. BINGIN

Bali's shortest, most makeable tuberide, best at mid to low tides. Remember to pull off before the inside sucks dry. Bingin used to be "the last secret spot" in Bali, but now there is a paved road from Pecatu right to the cliff, and a string of thatch-roof warungs lining the beach, offering food, iced drinks, massage and souvenirs. Plus some great value accommodation options along the beach from Bingin to Dreamland. Unfortunately Bingin's tight take-off zone gets crowded very easily, with any more than 10 surfers, so try to encourage other surfers to take turns, and respect the local kids who surf here.

Above: Bingin warung view. Photo by Emiliano Cataldi. Below: Stuart Thomas Bingin tube, photo by Shane Peel.

# IMPOSSIBLES                    DREAMLAND

**Impossibles** is well named. Renowned for high-speed tube runs, but sooner or later it will race past you. Sometimes though it lines up perfectly, usually on giant swells at dead low tide. You can either paddle out from Padang or Bingin.

**Dreamland** has a fun right and left reefbreak off the cliff, best at mid to low tide. Plus a fun **beachbreak**. Very popular with European learners and sun-worshippers. Lots of cheap places to stay nearby. Quite a social beach to hang out day and night. On most full moons you can find all-night dance raves on the headland. Be careful you don't trip over the cliff.

Above: Impossibles, with Padang behind, and then Uluwatu, photo Pat Koroman. Below: Tom Bauer, www.surfingthenations.com

## 04. BALANGAN

**Balangan** is a very fast left reef break, best on the highest or lowest tides of the month. Does not get too crowded, because most mid-tide waves tend to close out. Some surfers surf near the cliff, others surf the tail end. To get there turn right off the Uluwatu road into the road through the Suharto family owned "Pecatu Indah Resort". Balangan is probably Bali's most beautiful and clean white sand beach, a great place to relax for a day. There is an unusual temple half-way along the beach with statues hidden by magic black and white checked cloth, representing the eternal conflict and balance between good and evil. Balangan may close out every 50 metres or so, but that 50 metres can be the fastest buzz you've ever had! Wear your reef boots.

## 05. JIMBARAN BAY          06. AIRPORT RIGHTS & LEFTS

On big swells, a fun kid's beachbreak appears at high tide on the inside of **Jimbaran Bay**, near the seafood restaurants. But the quality wave here is **Airport Rights**, a hollow right reefbreak out near the southern end of the airport. You can get an outrigger from Kuta Reef to drop you off and pick you up later, but you need 6 foot plus of solid swell, a high tide and virtually no wind.

**Airport Lefts** is the first reef to the north of the airport, always bigger than the more famous **Kuta Reef**, but not as hollow. It still offers high tubes and a workable shoulder though. There are two distinct takeoff peaks, so choose your waves carefully.

Airport Rights Photo: John Huddleston

Photo Peter Neely 1980

## 08. KUTA REEF

The first reef break you should try. Picture-perfect 50 to 100 metre rides. Best on **high to mid tide**, with swell 3 to 8 feet. Over 8 feet it doubles up for a very precarious ledgey takeoff. Low tide is often too shallow. Kuta Reef is always Bali's most crowded reef break, with locals and tourists alike, so show plenty of respect and friendliness. Also don't paddle too far inside, towards the first peak, because you can't make the wave from there and locals will drop in on you every time. Try to take turns and share.

You can paddle out in 20 minutes, but it's better to pay locals a few dollars for a return **jekung** boat ride, available on the beach at Discovery Kartika Plaza Hotel, or at the end of **Jalan Kartika Plaza**. If Kuta Reef is too crowded, you can paddle 50 metres south towards the airport to **Second Reef**, a fun short left, or on bigger days maybe paddle way out to try **Secrets**.

NOW

**baliwaves**

Tawan, Kuta Reef. Photo courtesy Jim Bristow. Baliwaves www.baliwaves.com

## 09. KUTA BEACH BREAKS

The softest sand-bottom waves in Bali. Usually the smallest waves on the island, so **Kuta** is the best place for beginners and less experienced surfers. The long fast walls are a fun and exciting alternative to the dangers of surfing over sharp coral reefs. **High tide** is usually better, with peaks starting from out front of the **Hard Rock Hotel** all the way to **Legian** 2Km north. **Halfway** is the most consistent peak, opposite the Istana Rama Hotel, about 50 metres north of Poppies Lane 2. With a 6 foot plus swell on dead low tide, Halfway delivers superb sand-dredging tubes for the experts. You can rent surfboards, chairs and umbrellas on the long stretch of beach from Tuban to Kuta, to Legian and Seminyak. You can get lessons from the **Surfer Girl Surf S'Cool**. Crowds of Japanese and Balinese surfers flock to Halfway every day, so if it's too crowded walk a few hundred metres north to where there is often an uncrowded bank just before **Jalan Melasti**. If Kuta is too small, Legian is always at least 2 feet bigger.

www.BaliSurfReport.com

Tipi Jabrik, Legian. Photo courtesy Oakley

**High tide** at Legian can serve up some of the most power-packed beachbreaks in the world. Always bigger than Kuta, although it usually closes-out on low tide. It also closes out on high tide if the swell is over 8 feet. Because Legian is in the curve of the beach, it collects the compressed energy of all swells. A much more powerful wave than Kuta, 2km further south along the sand.

If Kuta is only 3 foot, sometimes Legian can be magnificent at 4 to 6 foot. A handy hint is that Kuta Reef is often about the same size as Legian. A hot crew of young Bali locals surf here regularly, so smile, share and be friendly to enjoy your sessions here.

The first semi-permanent sand bank is at **Jalan Melasti**, near the Legian Beach Hotel. Often relatively uncrowded.The most consistent peak is at **Jalan Padma**, near the Bali Padma Hotel, which is almost always crowded at high tide. Lefts and rights peel from opposite banks towards each other for 100 metres, then join up right on the sand for a big air finish. Lots of fun. You can sometimes find less crowded peaks 200 metres further north, near the **Puri Raja Hotel** and **Double Six** beach.

Padma beachbreak, Legian. Photo: Tim Hain

# 11. DOUBLE SIX & BEYOND

This is the best area to avoid crowds and find fun beachbreaks to yourself.

There are over 5 kilometres of isolated beachbreaks stretching from **Jalan Double Six**, past Ku De Ta Restaurant and through to **Canggu**. A few rivermouths and inshore reefs can create good sand banks. This area is best on **high tide** with a small swell, except **Ku De Ta** which handles low tide. Don't surf here alone as the currents can be quite strong. The waves tend to close out on low tide and can be quite dangerous with strange rips and black magic vibes. Many unaware tourists drown here who mistakenly swim in deep rips trying to avoid breaking waves.

**Double Six** is the fashionable Euro-Hippie section of the beach, with the best parties and topless sunbaking. You can join the **Rip Curl School of Surf** by day, enjoy sunset cocktails at **Sea Side Restaurant**, then bungy jump at **AJ Hackett**, and party all night with the glitterati at the **Double Six** nightclub.

To find totally uncrowded surf, try exploring the remote beaches north of Canggu, past Tanah Lot Temple and around **Tabanan**.

**Seminyak** is the start of "the real Bali" away from the tourist influences of Kuta and Legian. Just past the **Oberoi Hotel** you will find the highly recommended beachfront restaurant named **La Luciola**. Opposite it is the **Petitinget Temple** where you're likely to find locals praying every day, and you may occassionally be lucky enough to witness spectacular cremations or other Bali Hindu temple ceremonies, often on the full moon.

The **Tanah Lot Temple** past Canggu is one of Bali's most important and picturesque. It is serenely situated on a small rocky island, cut off at high tide from the black lava sand beach. Sacred snakes inhabit nearby caves, protected by local priests. Every year devout Bali Hindus make a pilgrimage to Tanah Lot which makes a very impressive procession. Similar pilgrimages are made to Uluwatu and the many other major Hindu temples on this **"Island of a Thousand Temples"**.

Tanah Lot Temple

Gamelan

Hindu Priest

## BALI BEACHBREAKS - dry season, may to september

| | |
|---|---|
| HIGH TIDE | Check Legian first, up to 8 foot. Over 8 foot Legian closes out, in which case go to Kuta |
| LOW TIDE | Check Halfway Kuta first as Legian usually closes out at low tide, even on small swells |
| SMALL SWELL | Check Legian first, then maybe check Canggu which can be another foot or two bigger |
| BIG SWELL | Check Halfway Kuta first. Kuta handles the biggest swells, but rarely gets over 10 foot |

Photo Peter Cox www.balisurfreport.com

## 12. CANGGU & PERERENAN

Pronounced **Chahng-goo**. An absolute swell magnet, always 2 feet bigger than Kuta, so it gets crowded on small swells. To get there drive 30 minutes north of Kuta along Jalan Legian. Turn left at Kerobokan traffic lights, follow signs to "TPA Sampah Canggu" and then left to **Pererenan**. A superb right peak breaks over black lava rock, with two fun lefts nearby. It's a good intermediate break between the safety of the beachbreaks and the dangers of the coral reefs. The trade winds blow side shore by mid-morning, so be there at **sunrise**, on a **high tide** for the right, mid tide for the lefts. There are small hotels next to the break where you could stay overnight if you want to try to beat the inevitable crowds. The 2-storey Sunset Losmen has great views of the surf. Canggu only handles up to 8 or 10 feet maximum. You can find less crowded, easier waves at **Berawa Beach** by following the signs to the Tugu Hotel one kilometre south. Some people now refer to Berawa as "Canggu". There are also rumours of good beachbreak waves further north near Tabanan. Check it out and let us know what you find!

Tipi Jabrik, Canggu lip surgery. Photo courtesy of Oakley Indonesia

## 13. BALIAN

Pronounced "**Bali-ahn**" which means "magic healer". A very peaceful rivermouth left and right peak, rolling for 200 metres over round river rocks. Cops heaps of swell, rarely under 4 foot and often bigger than Uluwatu, so gets crowded when small. It takes 2 hours driving from Kuta to Tabanan, on to Soka, then follow the coast 6km and turn left just past Sacred River Resort. Trade winds blow side-shore, so arrive at **sunrise**, or stay over night at the superb **Gajah Mina Resort**. There are rumours of other rarely surfed breaks nearby. Go exploring!

## 14. MEDEWI

Pronounced "**Mer-Day-wee**", but some surfers mispronounce it as "Ma-Dow-ee". A long left pointbreak, rolling gently over round river stones, a bit like a reversed Malibu. Perfect for **longboards** and intermediates. Can be a bit fat and slow, but still lots of fun. Best at mid to high tide, from 4 to 8 foot. Trade winds blow on-shore, so arrive at **sunrise**, or stay at the beachside cottages. About 3 hours north of Kuta. Swell here is usually larger than Kuta, smaller than Balian. There's also a fun right around the southern point too, so go for a stroll.

baliwaves

# BALI SOUTH COAST
## all seasons - north or no wind

Green Ball, Photo: Dick Hoole

### 15. NYANG NYANG

Pronounced "**N-Young N-Young**". Always has swell, but usually too big to surf safely. Normally only visited when everywhere else goes flat as it is difficult to get down the dangerous goat track that winds down the cliff face.

Arrive early to get it glassy before any wind. A **right** reefbreak with a sometimes left on the opposite side of an extremely treacherous channel with some weird currents. Take plenty of drinking water and be careful you don't slip down the cliff. Save enough energy for the climb back up.

### 16. GREENBALL

Green Ball, on Bali's exposed south coast, is usually too big to surf. It has undergone massive changes since its early days as a remote "secret spot", with a highway leading to the huge **Bali Cliff** luxury hotel. Hundreds of steps lead down the steep cliff to a thick **right** reefbreak, good up to 8 feet, but often too big and very dangerous. A serious commitment needed.

The waves here are very powerful, facing directly into the open ocean. Arrive early before any wind. Be careful of the currents, especially as the tide goes out. Experienced surfers only!

Don't surf the south coast alone - there is no land between here and Antarctica

Nyang-Nyang, Photo Jon Huberman

# BALI EAST COAST
## wet season - december to march

Surfer Girl's Beccy Sheedy on a typical day for Nusa Dua - overhead, thick and powerful. 200 metre rides are common

Photo: Jon Huberman

## 17. NUSA DUA

Bali's most consistent **right** reef break, rarely under 4 feet, so your best option most days. Often the only place breaking for weeks in the wet season, so it can get somewhat crowded (50 surfers spread over **3 peaks** is not uncommon). Breaks about 1 Km offshore, so hire a jekung ride out and back (around $5) from **Surfer's Beach**, reached by driving past the Nusa Dua Golf Course and turning left just past the Aman Nusa Resort. Look for the Surfer's Beach sign or hire a local driver.

There is a zippy **left** next to the channel 500 metres north of Surfer's Beach, near the "two islands" that give Nusa Dua its name, and a right peak on the other side. But the real action is out front - way out the back. Thick, deep water, shifty peaks wrap into a series of bowls for long rides with lots of power and variety. Steep over-head takeoffs are often followed by thick tubes that lead to deep water fat sections before another bowl wraps in and throws out. Nusa Dua is the Sunset Beach of Bali.

A good tip for Nusa Dua is to take out your **big wave board** even if it only looks 6 feet from the beach (it could actually be 8 to 10). Nusa Dua can handle 20 foot swells, but it is rarely surfed over 12 feet, so take some brave friends if you want to give it a try. The reef is on the edge of some very deep water, so expect to do lots of paddling against the strong currents, especially as the tide rushes in. It's much easier on an outgoing tide. Be warned - the shifty peak will clean you up sooner or later, so be prepared with a strong new leg rope! Experienced surfers only once the swell gets over 6 feet.

On small days you can find hollow right peaks 100 metres further south, close to the headland, within sight of the Nikko Hotel. Intermediate level surfers can enjoy the smaller days (it'll still be head high on the sets). **High tide** covers the reef safely, but still wear boots. There are other reefs all the way around the exposed south of Bali to Uluwatu, but few access roads.

Photo: Mick Curley

Serangan, Photo: Tim Hain

## 18. SRI LANKA

A hollow right reef break in front of **Club Med** north of NusaDua. A long-walled fast outside section leads into a challenging final bowl that pitches way out and is guaranteed to tube you before suddenly spitting you out safely into deep water.

Usually 2 foot smaller than Nusa Dua, and more **protected** from southerly winds that sometimes chop up Nusa Dua.

Another fast right peels off the next channel north, but it is rarely ridden because it closes out eventually. There is also an unusual novelty-value wave at **Mushroom Rock** between Nusa Dua's two "islands" but only at high tide.

It could also be worth checking for breaks in the reef between Sri Lanka and the mouth of Benoa Harbour.

## 19. SERANGAN, Turtle Island

Probably the most popular wet season wave for intermediate level surfers. A great **right** and **left** reefbreak, just 15 minutes from Kuta, now accessible by car due to the filling in of Benoa Harbour. Works all day, on **all tides**, on all size swells. Consistent but therefore very crowded. But this means Nusa Dua is not so crowded these days, especially on the bigger days.

Now that Serangan and Keramas have become publicized, there are a lot more surf options during the wet season. The pro surfers typically head to Keramas for tubes, big wave riders head to Nusa Dua, and intermediate surfers love Serangan. There used to be a rusty shipwreck here with a crazy wedge peeling along the side. **Peter Crawford**, the late-great legend photographer and ten times world kneeboard champ, captured some insane photos of surfers barreled barely a foot away from the shiwreck's sharp barnacles. R.I.P. P.C. !

Serangan. Photo Jon Huberman

Hyatt Reef. Photo: Jon Huberman

## 20. HYATT REEF

A very long way from shore (2 Kms) so hire a **jekung** boat to take you out and wait while you surf. There have been reports of a huge shark that is said to cruise the break often, but that may just be the locals trying to scare us off a great but fickle wave. There are not many days here with ideal conditions.

You need virtually **no wind**, and a **high tide** to stop you drifting off the take-off spot. So early morning high tides are the best conditions. Right hand peaks shift around a bit, but if you're in the right place at the right time, it can be a ride to remember. A reward for a somewhat difficult location.

Hyatt Reef doesn't seem to get too crowded, unlike its more famous neighbour Sanur Reef, probably because it is so far from shore and susceptible to winds.

## 21. TANJUNG SARI

A couple of fun right and left reef breaks in front of the **Tanjung Sari Hotel** and the **Sanur beach markets**.

The **right** can get awesome at dead **low tide** with a big swell (wear your reef boots). It offers a very long and fast ride at low tide, but at high tide it tends to break into sections and is therefore rarely ridden by tourist surfers.

These days lots of the local Sanur kids learn to surf here on the small days, so if you paddle out practice your Indonesian on them and make friends.

Sanur's hotel beachfront has a totally different feel to Kuta, more sedate, but the town is renowned for **Black Magic**, and particularly aggressive locals at the main Sanur Reef break.

East Coast Bali. Photo: Mick Curley

# 22. SANUR REEF

One of the world's best **right** reef breaks when over 8 feet. But unfortunately fickle Sanur only breaks about **20 days a year**, because it needs a very big swell from the right direction. Only a few days each year get over 10 feet. Nusa Dua is far more consistent and reliable, so surfers rarely stay at Sanur.

For Sanur to be 6 feet, Nusa Dua usually needs to be over 15 feet, depending upon swell direction. Under 4 feet Sanur sections badly and is dangerously shallow. From 5 to 8 feet it gets good but **very crowded,** with locals dominating. When it hits 10 feet it is a sight to behold as long-time Sanur devotees draw speed lines on 8 foot guns for 200 metres. Many surfers just live for those precious few days a year when Sanur pumps. Some say it is in the top 10 waves of the world, while others say it breaks far too rarely to be even considered, a bit like the freight train rights of Maalea in Hawaii.

If you get to surf Sanur over 8 feet you can really count yourself lucky! But be warned - it is best to pull out before the inside dredge-out or you could end up in Denpasar hospital, if you survive. The nearest doctor is conveniently located just 100 metres away at the Grand Bali Beach Hotel.

Local ferries leave from Sanur Beach for **Nusa Lembongan** Island most mornings if there is a high tide.

The classic seventies surf movie "Free Ride" showed one incredible tube ride at Sanur - Wayne Rabbit Bartholomew back-doored the dreaded inside dredge-out section. Ten feet behind the lip, dry coral reef right next to him, with no escape for over 50 metres. The tube sucked up so much water, he was actually surfing below sea-level (with his heart in his mouth!). He made it, but we don't know if he tried it again.

Even a master tube rider like Rabbit admitted he was terrified, and few people even attempt this horror end section. Reports say it is only makeable in 12 foot swells, but the consequences of a wipeout onto dry coral at that size are just too horrible to contemplate. But it looks so tempting...

Indo Surf & Lingo author Peter Neely tried for it on an 8 foot day in 1979 but had to prone out, scraping his single fin on the shallow coral before being picked up and thumped into the reef. Three discs in his back were cracked and his legs went numb for 10 minutes. But Sanur is still his favorite wave.

Sanur is a great wave to watch if the crowd gets too much. There is a good restaurant right in front of the break on the sand called 'Sunrise'. You can rent outriggers for a relaxing sail, or waterski in the lagoon with a motorboat from the **Grand Bali Beach Hotel**.

Tipi Jabrik, Sanur. Photo: Tim Hain

## 23. PADANG GALAK

Rivermouth beach break with boiling hot black volcanic sand. Best at **high tide** up to 6 feet, depending upon sandbars. Beware of polluted river water and board breaking shore dump. Gets fairly crowded with Japanese surfers and Sanur locals. Hard to find, so hire a local driver to take you.

## 24. KERAMAS

"**Golden Monkey**" was a well-kept secret for 20 years, but a new road changed all that. A very hollow pitching right, peeling off a black lava ledge, a bit like Off The Wall. Gets very crowded with hot locals and visiting pros. There are a couple of beach breaks on the walk in to avoid the crowds.

## 25. LEBIH

About 1 hour's drive from Kuta. "**Black Magic Point**" is a very sucky right lava-bottom ledge, on a black sand beach. Needs a big swell. At high tide it only closes out half the time - at low tide you'd be crazy to even try. A tube junkie's delight. The east coast still has unexplored surf potential, so maybe try driving down any road heading to a beach, or hiring a boat to cruise around the bays. Good luck!

## 26. PADANG BAI

Rumours of a good right hand point break peeling into the mouth of the harbour. But it needs a **giant swell** to even break, and you could be driving past excellent 8 foot Sanur to get it at possibly 4 feet, but you might also be the only surfer there. About a 2 hour drive from Kuta. The harbour water can get quite polluted with oil and diesel, so bring soap and shampoo to wash off after surfing here.

## BALI WET SEASON: QUICK SURF CHECK - october to april

SMALL SWELL
Check Nusa Dua first, because it collects all available swell and is rarely under 4 foot
If the wind is too south, check Sri Lanka. Serangan and Keramas get more swell, but more crowds too.

BIG SWELL
Take your gun to Nusa Dua! If it's too big, try Sri Lanka, then Turtle Island or maybe Sanur.
If Sanur is too crowded, check Tanjung Sari or Hyatt Reef. Or try exploring further north?

Ketut Menda, Padang Galak beachbreak. Photo: Piping

Keramas, Photo: Hilton Dawe courtesy Billabong

BILLABONG.

Lacerations

Lacerations, Photo Troy Sinclair, batukaranglembongan.com

Lacerations

Darren Roff, Lacerations by Piers Bradley,

Keramas

Lee Wilson, Keramas. Photo Tim Hain - Robert Wilson

This is what you dreamed Bali would be like - living right on the sand of a quiet, palm-fringed beach! Nusa Lembongan's beaches have no paved roads or cars to detract from the peaceful idyllic lifestyle enjoyed by the local fishermen for centuries. You can really relax and slow down here, beach combing for hours as you wait for the tide to come in and the surf to start pumping.

Dry season south-east trade winds are offshore at Nusa Lembongan, the same as Kuta in Bali. Low budget surfers catch the early morning public boat from **Sanur**, a two hour motor-sail over some of the world's deepest waters near the Lombok continental divide. Be prepared to get wet and sunburnt. Book through **Perama**, www.peramatour.com. Or relax on a luxury air conditioned cruiser from **Benoa** Harbour with **Bounty Cruises**, $35 one way. To get there fast, in 30 minutes by speedboat, go from **Sanur** with **Scoot** - www.scootcruise.com, or from Benoa with **BlueWater Express** - www.bwsbali.com

**Shipwreck** is the best break, a reliable right hand reef break that often increases in size with the tide, from 2 feet at low tide to 6 or even 8 feet on **high tide**. The tidal currents can be very strong, sucking you towards the remains of the rusting shipwreck as the tide rushes in, then the opposite direction as the tide rushes out. Waves here rarely get below 4 feet (on high tide). There are great bungalows on the beach, from cheap to luxury, all with great views of the action in the surf and the magnificent sunsets over Bali's Gunung Agung volcano.

**Lacerations** is the next reef break south, another right hander but much faster, hollower and far more viscious. It is not called Lacerations for nothing. An extremely shallow reef, definitely for experts only. Wear protective boots and vest. A Gath helmet is not out of the question either. Sometimes a left almost holds up on high tide, called **Razors**, but it is ultra fast.

The last break in the protected south corner of Lembongan is the aptly named **Playgrounds**, a fun left with a shorter right off the same peak. Great for longboards and SUP.

**Cheningan**, pronounced 'Chen-ning-ahn' is the next small island to the east before Nusa Penida, with a fun left point break ideal for longboards, but only when Nusa Lembongan is virtually too small to surf.

There are lots of places to stay along the beach, from basic $10 a night losmen to $500 a night luxury resorts. We can recommend **Lembongan Island Beach Villas** from $200 for a 2 Bedroom Villa - www.lembonganbeachvillas.com, Chris de Aboittiz's **Playgrounds Lembongan** $70 - www.playgroundslembongan.com, **Coconuts Beach Resort** $49, and ultra-luxury **Batu Karang Resort** from $300.

**Surf Travel Online** in Kuta can organize transport and hotel packages for all budgets - phone 750 550. Also check **The Perfect Wave** - www.theperfectwave.com.au

**Shipwreck**. Photo: skatergoris.com courtesy of www.batukaranglembongan.com

Playgrounds. Photo: Sky, www.bali-surfing.com

Lacerations, by skatergoris.com - batukaranglembongan.com

Razors. Photo: Piping - BSP Bali Surf Photography

# WHERE WILL WE SURF TODAY?

On the next few pages is a simple guide to where your best chance of a good surf in Bali might be. Depending upon lots of variables such as swell direction, increasing or decreasing swell, tidal movement, weather fluctuations etc, the wave size will probably vary a little from this guide. But you will still find it helpful as a starting point for **where to check out first**.

Naturally we can't guarantee the wind won't swing sideshore before you drive the 2 hours to Medewi for instance, or that the swell direction will suit the other side of the island. But hopefully this guide can help you make your own decisions on where you might get the best possible waves that suit your level of ability, while also hopefully avoiding the crowds.

### THE CROWDS

The object of this guide is to help spread out the crowds among the many already publicized breaks in Bali. Over the years surf magazines have featured photos of most of the places listed, but this guide tells you when they work best.

### SECRET SPOTS

There are not many secret spots left in Bali, so out of respect for those hardy souls who discovered and kept them secret, this guide book keeps them secret too. If you get to share a secret spot with a friendly local, keep it a secret!

Check out the **Legian** beachbreaks first and then consult these pages for the possible surf conditions elsewhere. The biggest waves usually will have the biggest crowds, but not always, so you decide where you'd like to try first.

### THE TIDES

The secret to scoring the best possible surf in Bali is to know which tides suit each particular break. We recommend you download one of our **Free Bali Tide Charts** from our website **www.indosurf.com.au**. Do it well before you go, so you can plan your trip around the best tides. You can also get them from most surf shops in Bali, and Tubes Surfers Club in Kuta.

### WAVE HEIGHTS

The measurements used in this book are for **Wave Face** height, from the trough to the crest. This is how we measure waves:

3 feet is waist high. 6 feet is head high.
12 feet is double overhead.
If you get lip-launched over the falls at Uluwatu, and you fall 10 feet before hitting the water, you deserve to call it 10 foot!

Photos: Ganti @ Padang, and Mick @ Bingin by Jon Huberman; Legian girls by Rip Curl School of Surf; Tube by Paul Kennedy

# BALI WAVE SIZE PREDICTION CHART
# DRY SEASON HIGH TIDE: may-september

## Legian Beach

### HIGH TIDE Offshore Wind

0-1' Legian - drag out the longboard!

## Possible surf size elsewhere

| Legian Beach | | Spot | Size | Notes |
|---|---|---|---|---|
| | | *GREEN BALL | 2-3' | Maybe? Certainly worth checking if no wind |
| | | NYANG-NYANG | 2-3' | Maybe? Certainly worth checking |
| | | ULUWATU | 1-2' | Probably too small, long waits between sets |
| | | CANGGU | 1-2' | Will be very crowded, inconsistent maybe |
| | | BALIAN | 1-3' | Collects almost as much swell as Uluwatu |
| HIGH TIDE | 2-3' *LEGIAN | *ULUWATU | 3-5' | Peak may be good at high tide |
| Fun beachbreaks | | BALANGAN | 2-3' | Worth a look if Ulu is too crowded |
| | | KUTA REEF | 2-3' | Might not be big enough, long waits between sets |
| | | CANGGU | 2-4' | Right should be good, but very crowded |
| | | BALIAN | 3-4' | Could be good, but needs no wind |
| HIGHTIDE | 4-5' *LEGIAN | *ULUWATU | 6-7' | Peak very good, but will be crowded |
| Great beachbreaks | | BALANGAN | 4-5' | Might not be too crowded |
| | | BINGIN | 3-5' | Better at lower tide. Check DREAMLAND beachie |
| | | KUTA BEACH | 2-3' | Beachbreaks near Hard Rock - good fun |
| | | KUTA REEF | 4-6' | Good, but certain to be crowded |
| | | AIRPORT LEFTS | 4-7' | Good, maybe not as crowded? |
| | | AIRPORT RIGHTS | 3-4' | Swell getting in? Needs very light wind |
| | | *CANGGU | 4-6' | Right excellent, but will be crowded |
| | | BALIAN | 3-6' | Maybe bigger? Maybe not crowded? |
| | | MEDEWI | 3-4' | Could be real fun longboard waves |
| HIGHTIDE | 6-8' | *ULUWATU | 7-10' | Peak excellent. Pull out the semi-gun! |
| Maxed out Legian | | PADANG | 5-7' | Just starting to break properly. Expect a crowd |
| | | BALANGAN | 6-10' | Could be awesome, maybe not crowded |
| | | BINGIN | 5-8' | Excellent on low tide, maximum size, crowded |
| | | *KUTA REEF | 6-9' | Great, approaching maximum size |
| | | AIRPORT LEFTS | 6-10' | Great, maximum size |
| | | AIRPORT RIGHTS | 4-6' | Could be awesome. Bigger the better |
| | | *KUTA BEACH | 5-7' | Very good beachbreaks |
| | | CANGGU | 6-10' | Rights excellent, maximum size |
| | | BALIAN | 5-8 | Maybe bigger? Or try MEDEWI? |
| HIGHTIDE | 8-10' | *PADANG | 7-9' | Excellent, your best bet. Experts only. |
| Closed out Legian | | IMPOSSIBLES | 10' + | Could be great as the tide goes low |
| | | KUTA BEACH | 6-8' | Excellent beachbreaks |
| | | KUTA REEF | 8-10' | Double up take-offs, but excellent |
| | | AIRPORT LEFTS | 8-12' | Maxed out, but could be great |
| | | AIRPORT RIGHTS | 6-8' | Excellent but could be very crowded |
| | | BALANGAN | 8-12' | Excellent but could be very dangerous |
| | | BINGIN | 7-10' | Maximum size, maybe too big? |
| | | ULUWATU | 9-12' | Peak dangerous, but low tide excellent |
| | | CANGGU | 10' + | Rights maxed out, maybe too big? |
| | | BALIAN | 10' + | Maybe too big? MEDEWI maybe smaller? |
| HIGHTIDE | 10' PLUS | *PADANG | 9-12'+ | Excellent Padang tubes. But ultra crowded |
| Deadly Legian | | ULUWATU | 12' + | Dangerous. Check low tide Outside Corner |
| | | IMPOSSIBLES | 12' + | Could be great as the tide goes low |
| | | BALANGAN | 12' + | Probably too dangerous? Check the end section |
| | | BINGIN | 9' + | Maxed out. Wait for low tide maybe? |
| | | KUTA REEF | 10' + | Maybe out of control? |
| | | AIRPORT RIGHTS | 8' + | Excellent but could be very dangerous |
| | | KUTA BEACH | 8' + | Beachbreaks huge, take the kids to JIMBARAN |
| | | JIMBARAN | 2-4' | Fun beachbreaks for the kids. Safe. |
| | | CANGGU | 12' + | Out of control for sure |
| | | BALIAN | 10' + | Probably too big to handle, swinging wide |
| | | MEDEWI | 8'+ | Starting to get a bit too wild probably |

# BALI WAVE SIZE PREDICTION CHART
## DRY SEASON LOW TIDE: may-september

| Legian Beach | Possible surf size elsewhere | | |
|---|---|---|---|
| **LOW TIDE Offshore Wind** | | | |
| 0-1' Legian Beach | *GREEN BALL | 2-3' | Maybe?- Needs no wind |
| | NYANG NYANG | 2-3' | Maybe? |
| | ULUWATU | 1-2' | Probably too small for Racetrack |
| | CANGGU | 1-2' | Lefts might be OK. Maybe try BALIAN? |
| **LOWTIDE 2-3' Legian** | *CANGGU | 2-4' | Lefts from mid tide. Rights better on high tide |
| Fun beach breaks maybe on higher tide | *ULUWATU | 3-5' | **Racetrack** should be good at low tide |
| | BALIAN | 2-4' | Maybe bigger? Try MEDEWI too |
| **LOWTIDE 4-5' Legian** | *ULUWATU | 6-7' | **Racetrack** will be very good |
| Solid beachbreaks at Legian, | BALANGAN | 4-5' | Maybe too shallow at low tide? |
| but better as tide comes in | *BINGIN | 3-5' | Good at low tide. DREAMLAND too |
| | *CANGGU | 4-6' | Good lefts from mid to low tide |
| | KUTA BEACH | 2-3' | Beachbreaks better at higher tide |
| | KUTA REEF | 4-6' | Good from mid to high tide |
| | AIRPORT LEFTS | 4-7' | Good from mid to high tide |
| | AIRPORT RIGHTS | 3-4' | Maybe smaller? Swell direction? |
| | BALIAN | 3-6' | Maybe bigger? Swell direction? |
| | MEDEWI | 2-4' | Could be fun longboard waves |
| **LOWTIDE 6-8' Legian** | *ULUWATU | 7-10' | **Outside Corner** starting to turn on |
| Maxed out Legian even on high tide | *BINGIN | 5-8' | Excellent tubes. |
| | DREAMLAND | 6-8' | Excellent outside reef |
| | PADANG | 5-7' | Just starting to break |
| | *KUTA REEF | 6-8' | Maxed out - from mid-tide only |
| | AIRPORT LEFTS | 6-10' | Maxed out - from mid-tide only |
| | AIRPORT RIGHTS | 5-6' | From mid-tide only |
| | KUTA BEACH | 5-7' | Good beachbreaks at Halfway maybe? |
| | CANGGU | 6-10' | Lefts from mid-tide |
| | BALIAN | 5-7' | Maybe bigger? |
| | MEDEWI | 4-6' | Could be great hotdog waves |
| **LOWTIDE 8-10' Legian** | *PADANG | 7-9' | Excellent from mid to high tide |
| Closed out Legian | *ULUWATU | 9-12' | **Outside Corner** excellent |
| | BINGIN | 7-10' | Maxed out |
| | DREAMLAND | 8-10' | Excellent |
| | *IMPOSSIBLES | 8-10' | Excellent |
| | BALANGAN | 8-12' | Very dangerous |
| | *KUTA BEACH | 6-8' | Excellent beachbreaks maybe? |
| | KUTA REEF | 8-11' | Double ups, wait till mid-tide |
| | AIRPORT LEFTS | 8-12' | Maxed out , wait till mid-tide |
| | AIRPORT RIGHTS | 8-10' | Very dangerous |
| | CANGGU | 10'+ | Lefts maxed out |
| | **JIMBARAN BAY** | 2-4' + | Inside beachbreak for kids |
| | BALIAN | 8' + | Maybe very good? MEDEWI? |
| **LOWTIDE 10' PLUS Legian** | *PADANG | 9-12'+ | Excellent but very dangerous |
| Deadly Legian | *ULUWATU | 12'+ | **Outside Corner** awesome |
| | BINGIN | 9'+ | Maxed out - check Impossibles |
| | *IMPOSSIBLES | 10' + | Excellent |
| | KUTA BEACH | 8'+ | Beachbreaks excellent maybe |
| | KUTA REEF | 10'+ | Closed out |
| | AIRPORT LEFTS | 12'+ | Closed out |
| | AIRPORT RIGHTS | 12'+ | Dangerous. Maybe from mid-tide |
| | JIMBARAN BAY | 12'+ | Outside cloudbreaks maybe worth trying? |
| | **JIMBARAN BAY** | 3-4' + | Inside beachbreak for kids |
| | BALIAN | 10'+ | Out of control probably. MEDEWI too big? |

# BALI WAVE SIZE PREDICTION CHART
## WET SEASON ALL TIDES: october - april

| Legian Beach | Possible surf size elsewhere | | |
|---|---|---|---|
| **ONSHORE WIND All Tides** | | | |
| **0-1' Legian** ALL TIDES | * GREEN BALL | 2-3' | Maybe? Also try NYANG-NYANG |
| | NUSA DUA | 1-2' | Maybe? Depends upon swell direction |
| | PADANG GALAK beach break | 1-2' | Maybe? Depends upon swell direction |
| **2-3' Legian** ALL TIDES | *NUSA DUA | 3-5' | Best at lower tide when small |
| | SERANGAN | 1-2' | Maybe too small? |
| | PADANG GALAK | 1-2' | Maybe? Swell direction? |
| | KERAMAS | 2-3' | Maybe? Swell direction? |
| **4-5' Legian** ALL TIDES | *NUSA DUA | 5-7' | Mid- to high-tide better with size |
| | *SERANGAN | 3-4' | Two fun rights and one fun left |
| | *KERAMAS | 3-5' | **Everywhere** should be great at this size! |
| **6-8' Legian** ALL TIDES | *NUSA DUA | 6-10' | Excellent long rides. Break out the gun |
| Maxed out Legian | SRI LANKA | 5-7' | Best mid-tide. More protected from south wind |
| | SERANGAN | 5-7' | Fun, but probably crowded |
| | *KERAMAS | 4-8' | Excellent, but the most crowded for sure |
| **8-10' Legian** ALL TIDES | *NUSA DUA | 8-12' | Incredible, bring your biggest gun |
| Closed out Legian | HYATT REEF | 6-8' | Excellent,  maybe less crowded? |
| | SERANGAN | 7-9' | Excellent, but probably crowded |
| | SANUR | 4-6' | Only just starting to turn on |
| | KERAMAS | 8-10' | Could be getting out of control |
| **10' PLUS Legian** ALL TIDES | NUSA DUA | 12' + | Sunset Beach style - Heavy! |
| Closed out Legian | *SRI LANKA | 9' + | Excellent ultra-hollow barrels |
| Cloudbreaks appear on horizon | HYATT REEF | 8' + | Excellent, maybe less crowded? |
| | TANJUNG SARI | 8' + | Low-tide could be very good maybe? |
| | SERANGAN | 8' + | Excellent but certainly crowded |
| | SANUR | 6' + | Starting to become Very Good maybe? |
| | PADANG BAI | 4-6' | Maybe bigger? Go exploring! |

**PADANG GALAK**, KETEWEL, KERAMAS, GUWANG and LEBIH also have **beach breaks** depending upon swell direction and sand buildup
There are a few other remote beaches up east, so go explore! But if you find any secret spots, please keep them secret.

The ancient Hindu religious symbol for Om, which in Balinese is called Ongkara. An excellent good luck charm or tattoo. But please do not place this holy symbol in inappropriate places.

Inspired by the eyes he saw on traditional Balinese fishing boats in 1973, Mitchell Rae designed his trademark Outer Island "Spirit Eyes", giving his surfboards a sense of life and high spirituality.

# OUTER ISLAND SECRET SPOTS

Rewards of The Search. Photo Ted Grambeau courtesy of Rip Curl

**RIP CURL**

Most surfers recognize that "**secret spots**" should be respected and protected. Before guidebooks and surf magazines came along, the only way to find out about new surf spots was by word of mouth. So we honour that tradition and respect the many secret spots in Indonesia. Our policy is to only mention places that have already been published elsewhere.

However, you will find that this book guides you to many relatively well-known spots where **the true locals** will be only too happy to take over and fill you in on all the latest discoveries nearby. Armed with the language lessons in the book, you'll soon find it easy to explore off the beaten track to discover your own perfect uncrowded waves. So start learning that lingo now!

The early surf explorers of the 60's and 70's tried to keep Bali, Java and Nias secret for many years, but these days Uluwatu, Grajagan and Lagundri Bay can be very crowded, and have lost much of the unique magic of the early days.

An unwritten **Code of Secrecy** has evolved for surf explorers not to divulge newly discovered surf spots, preserving them so we can all benefit by returning year after year to experience the uncrowded perfection. Don't destroy what you came to enjoy.

Indo Surf explorers are a unique breed of individual who cope with unimaginable hardships to find their little piece of paradise, so they deserve our respect and admiration. Please respect and protect these Secret Spots.

If you "discover" a perfect surf spot, please remember that most likely you are not the first surfer to enjoy the uncrowded waves, and you should leave it as you found it, a delightful "secret spot" for some other hardy adventurer to stumble upon and enjoy. Keep any discoveries a secret even from your best friends - just call it "Spot X, Somewhere in Indonesia". If they want to surf it, they'll have to take you along with them (all expenses paid of course) and sign The Oath of Secrecy!

With this in mind, here follows a little about each of the main Outer Islands of Indonesia, only naming the already publicized spots and describing the potential for new discoveries. There are a lot of Perfect Points throughout Indonesia waiting for you right now. Armed with the information and language lessons in this book, you'll be Out There in no time, exploring and discovering for yourself!

Remember: Leave only footprints, take only memories.

# LOMBOK

Lombok is a slow-paced island just as big as Bali but with much more coastline facing directly into the predominant swell direction. Bay after bay offers protection against the winds. Although close to Bali, crowds are much lighter. And most breaks suit intermediate level surfers. Except one...

The best known wave in Lombok is **Desert Point** on the southwest tip, "The Best Wave in the World" as voted by Australia's Tracks magazine readers. Incredibly long rides, tubing relentlessly over very shallow coral reef. Ten second tubes are possible. The winds blow offshore all dry season, from May to September.

Deserts is great for tube-loving goofy footers but difficult on your backhand. There is rarely a safe pull-out into deep water at the end, rather it just gets bigger and faster until it closes out over very sharp coral. Wear your reef boots, wetsuit and Gath helmet at low tide. Desert Point is definitely for the most experienced surfers only!

There are only a few rough boatsheds on the beach, with no toilets or water. Although hardcore guys sometimes camp out here, most surfers prefer to sleep aboard comfortable yachts chartered from Bali. See our **Trip Planner** page **16** for details.

Desert Point needs a solid ground swell to break well, and is renowned for long flat spells. Sometimes it is only ridable for a few hours each week. The tidal surge here is incredible because of the extremely deep water in the Lombok straits.

There are many other spots more easily accessed by yacht, motorbike or car. You can rent a car at the airport, Lembar ferry port, or in Mataram city.

**Surf Travel Online** can transport you from Kuta Bali to the quiet fishing village of **Kuta Lombok**, a great base for surf exploring with cheap losmen right on the beachfront ($10 to $25 a night). There are a dozen reefs within an hour's drive of Kuta, all good on their day, with a choice of good waves no matter what wind direction or swell size. Blue Water Safaris and Mahi Mahi take you from Bali to Lombok via Lembongan for around US$30.

The closest, most consistent spots are **Grupuk** and **Mawi**. Unfortunately theft is a problem in Lombok, so it is best to travel with local surf guides, lock your car and never leave anything valuable on the beach. Mount Rinjani has been particularly dangerous. Lombok has many breaks that can be uncrowded during the wet season, so go exploring for right handers!

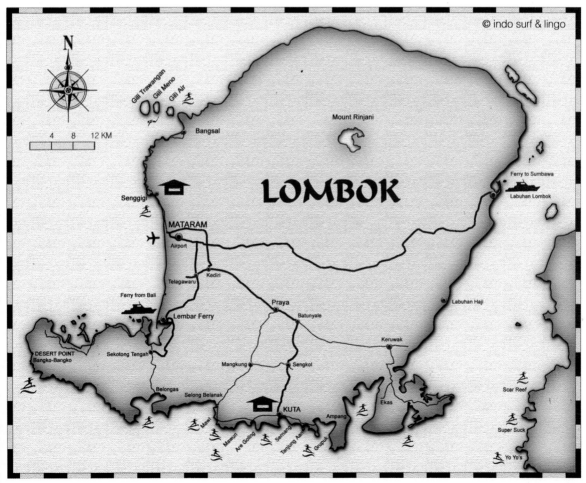

© indo surf & lingo

Gili Trewangan: JS Callahan/ tropicalpix

Desert Point reef dance: Jon Huberman

Desert Point. Photo: Mark Newsham

Desert Point. Photo: Jason Reposar

52

## LOMBOK - Quick Surf Guide

| | |
|---|---|
| **START** | Base yourself at Kuta Lombok - cheap rooms with good food right on the beach<br>There is a good choice of waves on all winds 10 to 60 minutes drive east or west of Kuta |
| **BREAKS** | East: Serneng, Tanjung Aan, Grupuk, Ekas. West: Are Goling, Mawun, Mawi, Silung Blanak, Deserts<br>On giant swells check out Desert Point, Sengiggi and maybe even Gili Air or Gili Trewangan |
| **WHEN** | All year OK, but early season often better with lighter winds - April to June maybe? |

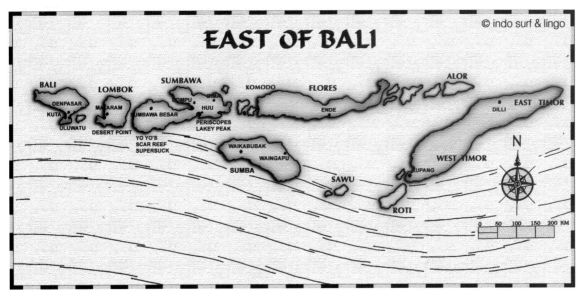

© indo surf & lingo

# EAST OF BALI

# SUMBAWA

Scar Reef - Cory Scott

Over 100 kilometres of surf potential. The south west tip of the island has consistent waves reached overnight on 10 night yacht charters from Bali, ideal if want to surf all the best breaks quickly. See Page **17**. New roads and hotels make travelling overland a good option as well, suited to those surfers with more time to experience the less crowded waves of Lombok and Sumbawa on a low-budget overland trip. Or stay in style at the **Nomad Tropical Resort** which has a long, easy left pointbreak straight out front. You will find offshore winds here or nearby all year through.

There are a few basic losmen from around $25 but they are a bit further from the surf - at Sekongkang near YoYo's, or Maluk near Scar Reef. Fly direct to **West Sumbawa** airport, or by bus from Lombok's Sweta terminal in Mataram. Head south to Taliwang, then to Maluk or Sekongkang.

**Yoyo's** offers a choice of two ultra-consistent fun rights, open to all swells but sometimes blown-out by dry season trade-winds that blow hard most afternoons. You can stay just 10 minutes away at the Nomad Tropical Resort, making it easy to get there early for glassy morning perfection.

**Scar Reef** and **Supersuck** are up the coast from Yoyo's, both seriously powerful left reef breaks with hundred metre long rides. Supersuck is offshore most of the dry season, but needs a big swell to break. Also check **Little Bingin**.

Lakey Peak - Cory Scott

The waves in **East Sumbawa** are excellent. Head to Hu'u, three hours drive from **Bima airport**. There are great waves with plenty of good losmen right on the beach at **Lakeh** (pronounced Lah-kay). **Aman Gati** is probably the best. With rooms for over 100 surfers, Lakey gets crowded in July and August, even though the winds are often sideshore at that time of year. Early season is much better. The rainy season often sees uncrowded glassy morning sessions, but it can also get very wet and stormy for days on end.

**Lakey Peak** is a perfect left and right pyramid-shaped peak, with the left usually the better ride. Predictable tubes, best at lowtide before the trade winds get up. **Lakey Pipe** is a sucky left ledge - high tide only, great for bodyboards.

**Nunga's** is the least crowded spot, a long thick left with many sections that handles any size swell. Great on big swells, when everywhere else closes out. When small, Nunga's can be great fun, ideal for intermediate level surfers, not too hollow or dangerous.

Two kilometres along the beach to the west of Lakey's is **Periscopes**, a great right tubing over a shallow rock bottom, but only surfable at high tide. Trade winds blow sideshore, so try to be here for glassy **morning high tides**. The 45 minute walk from Lakey's seems to keep the crowds down. There are other semi-secret spots to both the east and the west, so go exploring, or simply invite some locals to take you surfing at **Cobblestones** early one morning.

Lakey Pipe - Cory Scott

Super Suck. Photo Mark Newsham

Nungas, Photo: Andrew Shield

Scar Reef

Supersuck

Periscopes

Yo-Yo's, Photo Larry Pierce

Yo Yo's

Lakey Peak, Photo Carl Stone

Lakey Peak

Yo Yo's, Photo Gory Spain

Yo Yo's

## SUMBAWA - Quick Surf Guide

START:        Easiest to base yourself at Lakeh first. Cheap rooms, good food, right on the beach -
              Outer island trips don't come any easier! Fly into Bima airport, 3 hours drive from Huu & Lakey
BREAKS:       Lakey Peak, Lakey Pipe, Nunga's, Periscopes. Secret spots to the east and west - go explore!
WHEN:         All year OK, but best early season because of lighter winds, April to June maybe?

# SUMBA

Tarimbang, aka Miller's. Photo: Paul Kennedy

**Sumba, Flores, Roti, Timor, The Spice Islands** and **West Papua** are the major islands further east with an incredible amount of unexplored surf potential. The cultures here are very different to the rest of Indonesia, so learn as much as possible from a good general guidebook such as Lonely Planet's Indonesia Travel Survival Kit.

Getting supplies of fresh food and clean water can be difficult in the poorer, more remote areas. Transport is slow and sporadic, so make sure you have plenty of time available for travelling through these islands. Get a 60 day Visa first. Not many surfers get to this area because of the hassles involved, but that makes it particularly appealing to the true Indo surf adventurer willing to put in the effort, reap the rewards, and keep the secrets.

The waves in most islands east of Bali are possibly better early season, from around **March to June**, before the strong southeast tradewinds kick in. Some breaks are even better in the wet season with north-west offshore winds, but the weather can be very hot, stormy, wet and uncomfortable. But you might make some incredible discoveries.

The best known wave in Sumba is **Nihiwatu** (aka "God's Left" or "Occy's Left"), 30km south of Waikabubak in central Sumba. Surfers in the know say it is Indonesia's best quality uncrowded wave. This is because only guests at the luxury Nihiwatu Eco-

Resort can surf here. Budget surfers used to stay a few kilometres away at Chief Metebulu's in Watukarere, but these days there is no access to the beach at Nihiwatu. There is another losmen 10km away at **Rua** which has OK surf in the mornings, but is less protected from south-east winds so gets blown-out often.

**Kalala**, 2km from Baing on the south-east tip of Sumba, has a surf and fishing resort with basic bungalows from US$35 a day, including great meals. **Mr David's** has 4 reef breaks, both lefts and rights, plus even a fun beachbreak. Dave moved here after helping organize the first Om Bali Pro in 1980. So you can imagine how good the surf is! **Manggudu Island** lies offshore, run by the surfing Finns, with a huge left reef and early morning right. Check **www.eastsumba.com** or Fax Dave: 62 387 61333

**Tarimbang** on Sumba's central coast has a great right hander (aka Miller's) with cheap losmen nearby, probably the best spot for surfers on a tight budget. The wave is 500 metres out to sea, so pay a local to take you out and back. A less radical wave suited to all levels of experience. **www.surftravelonline.com**

**Kodi** on the west coast has cheap losmen near good waves. The rest of Sumba is mostly inaccessible by road. There is heaps of surf potential, but it is easiest to explore by yacht which takes time. Be warned that Sumba's waves are very thick and powerful, so don't forget your big wave board.

# TIMOR & ROTE

Ricardo Pomar at Tarimbang Sumba, aka "Miller's Right", while legend surfer Mike Doyle watches on

Photo: Heri Sri Noa Noa courtesy www.freeline.com.au

FREELINE

Nemberala. The bigger it gets, the better it gets

www.rotesurfhouse.com

Nemberala Photo Heri Sri Noa Noa www.rotesurfhouse.com

Although West Timor does have some surf, most people head to **Rote**, a small island off the south west coast which has many excellent offshore island reefbreaks. **Freeline Indo Surf Adventures** offers the best yacht tours here, surfing Nusa, Ndao, Ndana, Doo, Rai Jua, Dana and other secret islands.

Rote's world-class wave is **Nemberala**, a long easier left reef, also known as **T-Land**. Malole Rote Surf House is right on the beach - www.rotesurfhouse.com. There are still some excellent secret rights and lefts nearby on Rote if conditions are right.

You can get a ferry to **Sawu** from Kupang, but it's much easier to surf all these islands onboard Freeline's **Sri Noa Noa** yacht. If you have the time to explore, the possibilities are almost endless through these "south east islands". Preparation is vital however to prevent wasting your time, so study your Indonesian language, get good roadmaps, nautical maps and weather information. Ask your Indonesian Consulate about permits to enter Timor and Irian Jaya. Check the latest political situation too before you go. At the time of writing, travel to West Timor is OK again, but always travel with caution, especially in Kupang city.

## NUSA TENGGARA (the south east islands): Quick Surf Guide

| | |
|---|---|
| START | Base yourself at Nemberala in Rote first. Good losmen, good food, right on the beach. Cheap flights from Darwin to Kupang, then island hop by yacht or ferry |
| TRANSPORT | Yacht tours get to more quality surf spots than trekking overland - they are a great way to check the area for the first time - www.freelinesurf.com.au. Public transport is slow and unreliable |
| WHEN | Possibly best with early season lighter winds - March to June maybe? |

# JAVA: G-LAND

Java is one of the most densely populated islands on earth, yet **Grajagan** nestles quietly in the depths of a thick jungle rainforest on Java's south-eastern tip. A unique freak of nature, it is without doubt the world's most awe-inspiring, **consistently overhead** left-hand reefbreak. Every goofy footer in the world should try to surf **G-Land** at least once in his or her life. You won't regret it.

Access to Grajagan is strictly controlled by the National Park rangers, so you can only stay at the camps with the necessary permits. Living in a bamboo tree-house, challenging Grajagan's very long, fast walls is the ultimate jungle adventure! If you want to see "The Best Left on the Planet" ridden by the very best surfers, check out the classic Quiksilver G-Land Pro videos. There are also great **rights** "around the corner" in the wet season, with camps now staying open, or accessible by fast boat from Bali.

## GRAJAGAN

| | |
|---|---|
| **WHERE TO STAY** | **Joyo's Jungle Camp**: World Surfaris Freecall Australia 1800 611 163; Joyo's Bali Ph 777 649. **Bobby's**: Surf Travel Co Aust Ph 02 9222 8870; Bali Ph 755 588. **Tiger Camp**: www.g-landlive.com |
| **WHEN TO COME** | April to October is offshore. The biggest swells usually come June to August. Bring a gun! |
| **DO** | Bring "extras" like books, cookies, chocolate, hiking boots, mossie repellent - tiger repellent! |
| **DON'T** | Don't go to G-Land if you can't cope with big, powerful tubes - and wipeouts! |

Speedies. Photo: John Hepler

Photo: JS Callahan tropicalpix

Speed Reef G-Land

WORLD SURFARIS

# CENTRAL & WEST JAVA

Java's wild south coast is pounded by tons of swell, but it's a long road trip from G-Land to the next quality break. **Pacitan** in Central Java has some heavy sucking reefs, and uncrowded beachbreaks. About 2 hours drive from Jogjakarta airport.

An eight hour drive further west brings you to **Batu Karas**, near Pangandaran in Central Java. There is an easy sand-bottom right pointbreak straight out from the **Java Cove Hotel**. Ideal for learners, intermediates and longboards. Early season is best, from January to June before the tradewinds blow too hard.

Four hours south of Jakarta Airport is **Cimaja**, a great right pointbreak 8 Km east of **Pelabuhan Ratu**. There are lots of reefs and points nearby, the best being **Loji** on a giant swell and **Suwarna** any time. For full details see **www.ombaktujuh.net**.

**Ombak Tujuh** is a very thick left peak, like a reverse Sunset Beach. It's a 30 minute mortorbike ride through jungle from Batu Besar losmen at **Turtles**, a fast hollow left. Ombak Tujuh gets very big, very often, so experienced big wave riders only!

You could also take the time to check out the uncrowded beach breaks west of Cimaja, from Cisolok to **Baya**.

Off Java's south west coast is **Panaitan island** with Indonesia's most perfect yet dangerous left reefbreak, **One Palm Point**. Ridiculously shallow, so wear all the rubber and helmets you can afford. Ten second tube rides are quite possible, but a high fear factor watching the reef below. Tucked inside the bay is **Napalms**, almost as hollow but shorter and less deadly.

Panaitan has other lefts and rights which are great fun, a lot less dangerous than One Palm. The rights get blown out in the dry season, so surf them at dawn: **Illusions** is 100 metres of speed. **Apocalypse Wow** is a lot like Backdoor Pipeline but no exit.

Some horrendous experiences have been endured here with unseaworthy local fishing boats breaking down, so you are much safer travelling on reliable charter yachts like **Just Dreaming**.

On the way back, you can sail past the island remains of **Gunung Krakatau**, the site of the largest volcanic explosion in recorded history. The tsunami waves created in 1883 were 120 feet high. Over 36,000 people died and 165 villages were destroyed. Eruptions still occur every year, so it is too dangerous to get close. Great sunsets from the mainland though. There is supposedly a wave on the edge of the active volcano, if you're crazy.

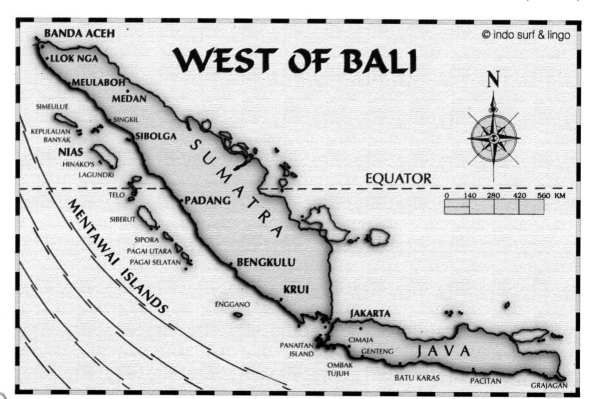

## WEST JAVA

| | |
|---|---|
| START | For lefts go to Turtles: www.freelinesurf.com.au. For rights go to Cimaja: www.ombaktujuh.net |
| WHEN | All year can be OK, but April to September is probably best. Batu Karas is better January to June. |
| TIP | Keep your feet up - lots of sharp urchins and shallow coral. Bring your reef boots. |
| BREAKS | Pacitan, Batu Karas; Cimaja, Turtles, Ombak Tujuh, Loji, Suwarna; One Palm, Apocalypse. |

Cimaja

Secret

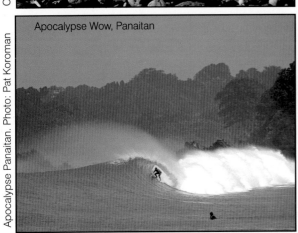

Apocalypse Wow, Panaitan

Pacitan

One Palm Point, Panaitan

Apocalypse Wow, Panaitan

Turtles

Ombak Tujuh

# SUMATRA
## the sumatran mainland

This is where some real hardcore surf discoveries still remain to be found, with many remote islands and wild jungle shorelines to investigate over the next few decades. Come up and get lost!

The **South Sumatra** coast has the best set up, with 10 quality waves in a beautiful area "like Bali 30 years ago". **Ujung Bocor** near Krui is known as "Sumatra's longest left", right in front of the **Ombak Indah** losmen. Fun for all levels of surfing ability.

**Way Jambu**, "the Sumatran Pipe" is 10 minutes south, as well as **Jimmys Right**, another very hollow wave for experts only. Quality uncrowded beach breaks are just 20 minutes north.

North Sumatra has good surf near **Banda Aceh** airport. The 2004 Tsunami destroyed most coastal villages in Aceh, with over 130,000 deaths and millions homeless. However the surf towns of **Llok Nga** and **Meulaboh** are now both re-open for business, and the local surfers will really appreciate you coming.

There is also good surf on **Simeulue**, the next large island north of Nias, with boats and planes leaving from Meulaboh or Medan. The 99 islands in **Kepulauan Banyak** (Many Islands) are best visited on surf charter yachts, surfing legendary spots such as **Treasure Island, Machine Gun Rights,** and **Bay of Plenty.** Or catch a slow ferry from Singkil to explore for yourself.

### SUMATRA

| | |
|---|---|
| START | Go to Krui or Aceh and the locals will be happy to share their waves if you show respect. |
| WHEN | Peak surf season in South Sumatra is the same as for Bali, from April to October |
| | North Sumatra is better early season, from January to July before the winds blow hard |
| BREAKS | Mainland - South: Krui, Bengkulu, the Sunda Straits. North: Banda Aceh, Llok Nga, Meulaboh. |
| | Nias - Lagundri, Indicators, Rockstars, Afulu, new West Coast spots. Go exploring! |
| | Outer islands - Hinako's (Bawa, Asu), Telo's, Mentawai's, Siberut, Sipora, Pagai, Enggano |

Aceh

Ujung Bocor

FREELINE

Sumatran Pipeline

View from your room

# NIAS
# lagundri

Nias suffered doubly with the 2004 Tsunami closely followed by the 2005 Earthquake. Eighty percent of the main towns were destroyed, with thousands left homeless. The famous **Lagundri Bay** reef lifted two metres, but the new break created further out is even better, hollower on all tides. Nine second tube rides!

It is much better to fly to Nias from Medan in 1 hour, rather than wasting days on the slightly cheaper ferry and bus option. Boraspati (+62 61 4526802) can book you onto daily Sutra or Merpati flights for around US$60. Widy Jet Boat or Pelni ferry from Sibolga might save you $20, but the ferry and bus takes 24 hours. The locals have built fresh new losmen along the beachfront, and surfers have flooded back there recently.

# hinakos

From Nias you can organize speed-boat day trips out to the **Hinako Islands**. Longer trips are possible, but the professional surf charters listed in this book are much safer and more comfortable than taking a chance with local fishing boats.

The right at **Bawa** and the left at **Asu** were lifted dramatically by the earthquake, but the new breaks are still awesome, seriously powerful hollow waves, best for experienced surfers. You can stay in style now at the **VIP Asu Villa** – www.vipasu.com

Ask around Lagundri for information about new discoveries nearby such as **Rockstars**. Everyone going to Nias should definitely seek the latest advice about **malaria** prevention.

Surfer Girls Martina @ Lagundri. Photo: Joe Hubermann

Lagundri. Phil Goodrich. Photo: Santosha Wau

Lagundri

Asu

SUMATRAN SURFARIIS

Lagundri

Lagundri Indicator

# MENTAWAIS

South of Nias are the famous Mentawai Islands, pronounced "Men-tah-why", without doubt **The Best Waves on the Planet.**

Most islands are covered in dense rainforest jungles, hardly any roads, limited food supplies, and only a few comfortable places to stay. Despite thousands of surfers coming here over the last decade, most surfers still prefer to return on a yacht rather than trekking overland, camping out, or going feral with the natives. New land-based resorts offer a touch of luxury and no seasick nights - www.**WavePark**.com, **AloitaResort**.com, **KanduiVillas**.com, **TogatNusaRetreat**.com, and **AuraSurfResort**.com

We recommend you travel with the experienced professional yachts listed in this book, and avoid unsafe local fishing boats, no matter how cheap they may seem. Safety first, always!

The Mentawai people are the most primitive, tattoo-covered natives in Indonesia. Many live a simple subsistence life in the jungle, based on bartering, not money. Often they can not supply you with food or water, no matter how much money you have. Most prefer to trade goods for knives, axes, fishing nets, or even beads and betelnut rather than cash. Animistic religions and black magic are still strongly believed in, despite the spread of Christianity. The natives believe all things possess a soul, from rocks to trees to rivers; illness is caused by upsets to the souls of the objects around us, so western medicines are non-existent here. Thankfully **Surf Aid** is doing something to change that - www.surfaidinternational.net

**Padang** is now the base for over 30 yachts travelling to the Mentawais. The exact location of most surf spots remains a closely guarded secret, so simply rely upon your yacht captain to guide you to the best breaks each day. The Mentawais has hundreds of waves, but only about 30 are surfed regularly

In the north there are a dozen waves in the **Telo** group alone, with the first resort virtually booked solid. The largest island of Siberut has fast, hollow lefts at **E-Bay**, thick intense right tubes at **Bankvaults**, excruciatingly long left tubes at **NoKandui**,

and even longer ones at Kandui Rights aka **Rifles** (600 yards of ultimate speed). Sipora Island has one of the world's best right tubes, **Lance's Right**, aka **HT's** or Hollow Trees. The pro surfers make it look easy in the videos, but in reality it is a very dangerous tube with a slab of almost dry coral called "The Surgeon's Table" awaiting any mishap. Not for learners. South Pagai Island has **Rags** Left and Rags Right, both ultra-long hollow tubes also for experts only.

On Pagai Utara island is **Macaroni's**, "the most fun high-performance left in the world". Maca's peels like a machine, but the take off is fast and hollow. The new resort has made surfing here far more comfortable - www.**MacaronisResort**.com.

One of the most consistent lefts is **Thunders** off Pagai Selatan. A long way south is **The Hole**, an ultra-nasty gaping chasm. Expert tube riders only. Plus many secrets down to **Enggano**.

Most Mentawai waves suit more experienced surfers. For **intermediate** level surfers, ask your captain to take you to the following breaks, which can be fun on smaller days: **Nipussi**, a consistent yet mellow right with 75 yard rides; **Four Bobs**, another fun 75 yard right; **Burgerworld**, the slowest, easiest 100 yard right; **Scarecrows**, a wedgey left take-off with an inside tube; **Lance's Left**, a more powerful left barrel to 100 yards; **Macaroni's**, take off wide for 100 yards of non-stop mechanical lip bashes; **Telescopes**, a perfect reeling left up to 500 yards; and **Thunders**, the most consistent left in the Mentawais, with a wider peak great for intermediate surfers on smaller days.

The **Andaman** and Nicobar islands north of Sumatra have very good reef surf, but are only accessible through India, where you must go through Indian Immigration. Don't chance taking a local fishing boat from Sumatra - you may be arrested, or even worse, pirated! This is dangerous pirate territory, especially after the destructive 2004 Tsunami and quakes.

*Special thanks to Anthony & Jordan of **Saraina Koat & Kandui Villas** for contributing their wave knowledge to this section.

Burgerworld, Photo courtesy Christie www.WavePark.com

SARAINA KOAT

Photos: Wave: Yassine Ouhilal. Faces: Yassine Ouhilal, Russ Hennings A-Frame, Kate Gerson

Kandui Left. Yadin Nichol, Photo: Yassine Ouhilal

WAVEPARK.COM

SUMATRAN SURFARIIS

wavepark.com

RIP CURL

NoKandui, Mentawais. Photo: Brian Nevins

Macaronis, Mentawais. Photo: Alan Van Gysen

Rifles firing, Mentawais. Photo: Brian Nevins

Rifles exploding, Mentawais. Photo: Brian Bielmann A-Frame

 LIVE THE SEARCH

# LEARN THE LINGO
## connect with the locals

The ISC Indonesian Surfing Championship top surfers for 2010. See these guys carving it up on **www.isctour.com**

**Open Pro Division**

1 Putra Hermawan

2 Made Dedi Dwi Santoso

3 Pepen Hendrik

4 Made Raditya Rondi

5 Lee Wilson

6 Marlon Gerber

**Open Pro Division**

7 Agus Frimanto

8 Dede Suryana

9 Mustofa Jeksen

10 Wayan Suprayitna

**Junior**

1 Jeren

2 Koko Mitsua

**Junior**

3 Mansur

4 Ediana Putra

5 Usman

**Pro-Junior**

1 Putra Hermawan

2 Agus Frimanto

3 Gazali Hamzah

**Pro Junior**

4 Darmaputra Tonjo

5 Putu Anggara

**Women**

1 Yasnyiar Gea

2 Dyah Rahayu Dewi

3 Febri Rahma Ningsih

4 Jasmine

**Masters**

1 Ketut Juliarta

2 Wayan Widiyartha

3 Ketut Wirtawan

4 Made Lapur

5 Wayan Budayasa

**2010 Indonesian Surf Champions**
Photos thanks to Tim Hain, ISC

# TEACH YOURSELF INDONESIAN

Learning the Indonesian language can be a relatively easy affair. Compared with English, the structure of Indonesian is far simpler. However, deciding where to get started can be a problem, so here are a few hints:

Don't try to learn too much all at once. Just a few words and sentences each day, so it will be easier to remember.

Start by practicing the "**Everyday Words and Greetings**" because this one page is the key to starting just about every basic conversation. Then you decide what you would like to learn next, after glancing through the rest of the book.

Perhaps you could copy the "Indonesian Pronunciation" main differences from English onto a sheet of paper and place it somewhere you will see it often (refrigerator? back of the toilet door?) Then maybe you could practice asking questions to find surf spots.

Test yourself by reading Indonesian into a voice recorder, then checking your pronunciation. Ask a friend to test you on each page of this book, or better still, learn with a friend. Two people learning together will be much easier and faster.

Next use **The Power of Visualization** to imagine yourself in Indonesia. Close your eyes and see yourself in situations that you will experience in the future. Prepare for those situations now. The speed at which you learn Indonesian is directly proportional to your need to do so.

For example, visualize yourself arriving at the airport perhaps, or a hotel, marketplace, idyllic palm-fringed beach or wherever you hope to visit when you go to Indonesia.

Imagine you strike up a conversation with a friendly local. Write in English a short, simple dialogue of the questions you may ask, and the answers you may receive.

Next, translate that dialogue into Indonesian by looking up new words in this book or your English-Indonesian dictionary "**kamus**". You may be surprised how much simpler and precise it will read in Indonesian.

Once you arrive in Indonesia, carry a pocket notebook and write down any new words you would like to learn. Look them up in your kamus that evening, and practice saying them. The next day, attempt to use the new words you learnt last night.

Don't be afraid to make mistakes, because they are an inevitable part of any learning process. The Indonesian people will happily help you learn their language with a good sense of humour. In fact, they will be your very best personal teachers.

Terms of respect towards adults are very important, as in most Asian cultures. Rather than saying "you", it is more respectful to use the person's name or family status - so often you will address adults as "Mother" or "Father", almost speaking to them in the "third person". eg. "Where is father going?" rather than "Where are you going?".

One of the key words you will use everyday is **Selamat** (pronounced **S'lah-maht**) which by itself can mean many things, such as "Cheers", "Good health", "Good luck", "Congratulations" or "Safe".

Combined with other words "Selamat" becomes "Good Morning", "Good afternoon", "Good night", "Good bye", "Good journey", "Bon Apetit", and other general blessings.

Selamat is similar in meaning to "Salam" and "Shalom" in other languages, in that it infers a blessing upon whatever activity you are undertaking. For example, the Indonesian term for "Good Bye" is "Selamat Jalan" which loosely translated means "May your road be blessed".

# EVERYDAY WORDS & GREETINGS

Learn just this one page and you're well on the way to holding a basic conversation. It's that easy!

| ENGLISH | | INDONESIAN | PRONUNCIATION |
|---|---|---|---|
| Good morning | = | Selamat pagi | (S'lah-maht pah-gee) Sunrise to 11am |
| Good day | = | Selamat siang | (S'lah-maht see-ung) 11am-3pm approx |
| Good afternoon | = | Selamat sore | (S'lah-maht sore-eh) 3pm to sunset |
| Good evening | = | Selamat malam | (S'lah-maht mah-lahm) After dark |
| Good night | = | Selamat malam | (S'lah-maht mah-lahm) |
| Good bye | = | Selamat jalan | (S'lah-maht jah-lahn) To person leaving |
| | | | Loose translation "Bless your road" Jalan = road |
| Good bye | = | Selamat tinggal | (S'lah-maht ting-gahl) To person staying |
| | | | Loose translation "Bless your stay" Tinggal = stay |
| "How are you?" | = | Apa kabar? | (Up-ah kah-barr) Literally: "What news?" |
| "I'm well" | = | Kabar baik! | (Kah-barr bike) Literally: "Good news" |
| **Thank you** | = | **Terima kasih** | **(T'ree-mah kah-see)** Literally: "Receive love" |
| Thank you very much | = | Terima kasih banyak | (T'ree-mah kah-see bun-yuk) |
| You're welcome | = | Kembali | (K'm-bahlee) Literally: "Returned" |
| Welcome | = | Selamat datang | (S'lah-maht dah-tongue) eg when arriving at hotel |
| **Sorry** | = | **Ma'af** | **(Mah-Uff)** |
| I apologise | = | Saya minta ma'af | (Sigh-ah min-tah mah-uff) |
| Excuse me | = | Permisi | (Purr-miss-ee) eg when leaving a home or |
| | | | when weaving through a crowd |
| **Please** (may I have) | = | **Minta** | **(Min-tah)** eg. when ordering food |
| Please (help) | = | Tolong | (Toe-long) |
| Please (try) | = | Coba | (Cho-bah) |
| Please (eg come in) | = | Silahkan | (Sil-ah-kahn) |
| What is your name? | = | Siapa nama anda? | (See-up-ah nah-ma undah) |
| My name is...(Name) | = | Nama saya...(Name) | (Nah-ma sigh-ah ....Name) |
| Where are you from? | = | Anda dari mana? | (Un-dah dah-ree mah na) |
| I am from...(Place) | = | Saya dari...(Place) | (Sigh-ah dah-ree... Place) |
| Where are (you) going? | = | Mau ke mana? | (Ma-oo k'mah-nah) Literally: "Want to where?" |
| Just walking | = | Jalan-jalan saja | (Jah-lahn jah-lahn sah-ja) |
| To the beach | = | Ke pantai | (K' pun-tie) |
| To the shop | = | Ke toko | (K' toe-koe) |
| Nowhere | = | Tidak kemana | (Tee-duck k'mah'nah) |
| Yes | = | Ya | (Yah) |
| No | = | Tidak | (Tee-duck) |
| Like | = | Suka | (Soo-kah) |
| Don't like | = | Tidak suka | (Tee-duck soo-kah) |
| Want | = | Mau | (Mao) |
| Don't want | = | Tidak Mau | (Tee-duck Mao) |
| Good | = | Bagus | (Bah-goos) |
| Very good | = | Bagus sekali | (Bah-goos s'kahlee) |
| Not good | = | Tidak bagus | (Tee-duck bah-goos) |
| Fine/ OK | = | Baik | (Bike) |
| Very fine | = | Baik-baik | (Bike bike) |
| Until (we) meet again | = | Sampai jumpa lagi | (Sum-pie (keeta) joom-pah lah-gee) |

# BAHASA INDONESIA
## a brief history & a few basic rules

Manners are very important to Indonesian people, and since you will be treated as an honoured guest in their country, it is only right you should learn how to repay that courtesy. So learn the basics "Please" and "Thank You" straight away. Believe me, you will be invited into many homes, offered many cups of coffee, and the lessons in this book will prove invaluable. New friendships will be quickly cemented, new surf spots will be revealed.

You will find the Indonesians happy to help you learn their language, freely offering insights into their customs and way of life. They will become Your Best Personal Teachers, so keep an open attitude to everyone you meet there, and ask their help with learning their language.

But first, a little about the history of this "made-up" language, a few basic rules and hints on pronunciation:

The Indonesian Language was created in 1929 as a means to unify the thousands of islands previously claimed by Holland as The Dutch East Indies. With over 250 different languages throughout the islands, it was necessary to have one unifying national language.

"Bahasa Indonesia" was based on Malay, the traditional language of seafaring traders in the region, but through the years has adopted many new words from Sanskrit, Dutch, Arabic, and more recently from English (and MTV).

Today Bahasa Indonesia is spoken by all educated Indonesians from the north of Sumatra, through Java, Bali and the south-east islands to Timor and Irian Jaya. Almost everyone speaks another "mother language" from birth, like Balinese, Javanese or Sumatran. They all have to learn Indonesian at school.

Basic Indonesian, as used by the majority of the population, is a simple language without many of the inconsistencies found in English. You can learn all the basics in this book.

There is **no** "**the**" or "**a**" in Indonesian, so to say "the Beach" for example, or "a Beach", you just say "Beach", or in Indonesian "Pantai" (Pun-tie).

Sometimes "this" or "that" can be used as an alternative for "the". Eg. "This Beach" = "Pantai ini" (Pun-tie in-nee) or "That Beach" = "Pantai itu" (Pun-tie it-too)

There is **no** "**is**" in Indonesian, the intransitive verb "to be", so to say "The beach is close" you just say "Beach close" = "Pantai dekat" (Pun-tie dec-kaht)

Plurals are often expressed by just doubling the noun. Eg "Beaches" is "Pantai-pantai". But the use of qualifying words that already imply plurality can be enough alone eg. "Many beaches" is "Banyak pantai" (Bun-yuk pun-tie).

Photo: David Pu'u

# TENSES

Tenses are handled simply by the use of a few adverbs to denote timing rather than conjugating the verb as in English. This is what helps make Indonesian so easy to learn! eg. The verb for "Go" - "Pergi" does not change:

| | | | | |
|---|---|---|---|---|
| Saya pergi | ke pantai | = | I go | to the beach |
| Saya sedang pergi | ke pantai | = | I am going | to the beach |
| Saya belum pergi | ke pantai | = | I have not yet gone | to the beach |
| Saya akan pergi | ke pantai | = | I will go | to the beach |
| Saya mau pergi | ke pantai | = | I want to go | to the beach |
| Saya sudah pergi | ke pantai | = | I have already gone | to the beach |
| Saya baru pergi | ke pantai | = | I just went | to the beach |

| | | | | |
|---|---|---|---|---|
| Sedang | (se-dung) | = | am | Present tense |
| Belum | (b'loom) | = | not yet | Future tense |
| Akan | (ah-kahn) | = | will | Future tense |
| Mau | (ma-oo) | = | want | Future tense |
| Sudah | (sue-dah) | = | already | Past tense |
| Baru | (bah-roo) | = | just | Past tense |

# TIMING

Timing can also be denoted by the words for "today", tomorrow", "yesterday" etc., or "earlier", "later", time and days of the week. Here are some examples:

| | | | | | |
|---|---|---|---|---|---|
| Saya pergi ke pantai | hari ini | = | I (will) go | to the beach | today |
| Saya pergi ke pantai | kemarin | = | I went | to the beach | yesterday |
| Saya pergi ke pantai | besok | = | I (will) go | to the beach | tomorrow |
| Saya pergi ke pantai | tadi | = | I went | to the beach | earlier |
| Saya pergi ke pantai | nanti | = | I (will) go | to the beach | later |
| Saya pergi ke pantai | jam satu | = | I (will go/went) | to the beach at | one o'clock |
| Saya pergi ke pantai | hari Minggu | = | I (will go/went) | to the beach | Sunday |

# CONSTRUCTING A SENTENCE

Sentences are constructed similarly to English, Usually with the subject first, then the verb, object and adjective. But please note: **Adjectives** usually come **after** nouns - to say "the big wave" you say "wave big" (ombak besar).

There are no Possessive words for "mine", "yours", or "ours" - just the usage of "me", "you" or "us" after the object denotes possession. So, "My surfboard" is stated "Surfboard me" ("Ski saya"). "My small surfboard" is said "Surfboard small me" ("Ski kecil saya").

Only for "his" or "hers" can this change by the addition of "nya" at the end of the word to denote ownership eg. "His surfboard" = "Skinya". However "dia" (he/she) is also very common eg. "Ski dia".

Note: You may hear some locals saying "ku" (shortened "aku" = "I") or "mu" (shortened "kamu" = "you") to denote ownership, but don't copy this fading habit as these are regarded as less polite than using "saya" or "anda".

An understanding of just these few rules will allow you to speak and understand the basic Indonesian spoken in most everyday situations and get you on the road to discovering your own surf spots.

Please understand that more formal, sophisticated levels of the language do exist, with their own complex rules of suffixes and prefixes, but for the average traveller to Indonesia, the basic rules outlined here are more than sufficient to get by, make friends and be understood.

The only other "rule" is that like all nationalities, the Indonesian people respond marvelously to politeness and respect - they really will appreciate your attempts to speak their language. Also remember that often just a smile will go a long way to creating the opening for better understanding and friendship.

# INDONESIAN PRONUNCIATION

The pronunciation of most letters in Indonesian is quite similar to their English pronunciation. But the most important differing ones have been highlighted on this page. Practice reciting the alphabet in Indonesian, just like as schoolkids we learnt our own English alphabet. Sing it if you like. But most importantly, memorise the sounds of the vowels **AEIOU** and the consonants **C** and **R** - they're very different to English!

## the letter — pronunciation & examples

| the letter | | pronunciation & examples |
|---|---|---|
| A | **AH** | Short "ah" as in "far" eg. "What" = "Apa" (Ah-pah) Never as in "bad" or "page" |
| B | Bay | Similar to English. Short sound as in "bingo" at the beginning of a syllable eg. "Good" = "Bagus" (Bah-goos). Pronounced "p" at the end of a word eg. "Fate" = "Nasib" (Nah-sip) |
| C | **Chay** | Always pronounced "CH" as in "channel", never "k" as in "candy". eg. "Candi Dasa" village in Bali is pronounced "Chahn-dee Dah-sa" |
| D | Day | Similar to English. As in "dingo" at the beginning of a syllable, but pronounced "t" at the end of a word, eg. "Alphabet" = "Abjad " (Ahb-jut) with a soft end. |
| E | **Eh** | Similar to "air". When stressed, sounds like "e" in "Net". eg. "Red" ="Merah" (Mair-ah). When unstressed, sounds like "e" in "The" almost swallowed. eg. "Raw" = "Mentah" (M'n-tah). "Margarine" = "Mentegah" combines both "e" sounds (M'n-tair-gah). Often, when two "e"s appear in a word, the first is unstressed and swallowed. |
| F | eF | Similar to English, though sometimes in words of Arabic origin, is pronounced "p" eg. "Think" = "Pikir" (pronounced "Fikir") |
| G | Gay | Similar to English, with a hard sound as in "go". Never as in "ginger" |
| H | Hah | More pronounced than English but slightly aspirated and extended, as in "hairy" |
| I | **Ee** | Like "ee" in "street", or slightly shorter like "i" in "pin". eg. "Bali" pronounced "Bah-lee" |
| J | Yae | Similar to English, with a hard "dj" sound as in "jack". eg. "Road" = "Jalan" (Jah-lahn) |
| K | Kah | Similar to English at the beginning of words with a hard sound like "koala", but not plosive. At the end of words however, almost silent eg. "Office" = "Kantor "(Kahn-tore), "Pretty" = "Cantik" (Chahn-tick) |
| L | eL | As in English eg. "Long time" = "Lama" (Lah-ma) |
| M | eM | As in English eg. "Bathe" = "Mandi" (Mahn-dee) |
| N | eN | As in English eg. "Later" = "Nanti" (Nahn-tee) |
| O | Oh | As in English "hot" eg. "Soup" = "Soto" (Soh-toe) |
| P | Pay | As in English eg. "Beach" = "Pantai" (Pun-tie) |
| Q | **Koo** | Rare, usually only for adopted English words. |
| R | Air | Always rolled as in French. eg. "First" = "Pertama" (Purr-tah-ma) |

| | | |
|---|---|---|
| S | eS | As in English. eg. " I " & " Me " = "Saya" (Sigh-ah) |
| T | Tay | As in English. eg. "Tofu" = "Tahu" (Tah-hoo) |
| U | Oo | As in "foot" or "put". Never as in "bucket" eg. "Ubud" village in Bali pronounced Oo-boo-d |
| V | Vay | Similar to English but rarely encountered. Sometimes pronounced "f" for ease |
| W | Way | As in English. eg. "Shop/kiosk" = "Warung "(Wah-roong) |
| X | eX | As in English, but very rare. |
| Y | Eegrek | As in English "yes" eg. "Yes" = "Ya" (Yah) |
| Z | Zet | As in English "zoo", but very rare. Sometimes changed to "j" sound eg. "Era" = "Zaman" (Jah-mahn) |

## dipthongs

| | | |
|---|---|---|
| aa | a'a | A slight gap should be inserted between the letters eg. "Sorry" = "Maaf " (Ma-af) with a gap. Each "a" is pronounced separately. |
| ai | aye | Like English "i" in "bike" eg "Beach" = "Pantai" (Pun-tie) |
| au | ow | Like English "ow" in "wow" eg. "Knife" = "Pisau" (Piss-ow) |
| ny | ny | Nasal sound as in English "New", pronounced as one sound eg. "Madam" = "Nyonya" (Nyon-nya) |

## vowels

| A | = | Ah | | E | = | Eh |
|---|---|---|---|---|---|---|
| I | = | Ee | | O | = | Oh |
| U | = | Oo | | | | |

**AEIOU**  =  **Ah, Eh, Ee, Oh, Oo**

## remember

C  = **CHay**          R  = **AIRrr**

## stress

Light Stress usually falls on the second last syllable of a word eg. "Pantai" is spoken as "PUN-tie".

The rare exception is words with the swallowed E in the second last syllable, where the Final syllable is then stressed eg."Besar" (Big) is stressed as "b-SARR".

Usually the most important word in a sentence is also lightly stressed to emphasise the meaning.

# PRONOUNS & COURTESIES

| | | | | |
|---|---|---|---|---|
| **I** | = | **SAYA** | (Sigh-ah) | Most used, recommended |
| I | = | Aku | (Ah-koo) | Only among friends |
| **You** | = | **ANDA** | (Ahn-da) | Formal, respectful |
| You | = | Saudara | (Saw-dahra) | Only among friends |
| You | = | Kamu | (Kah-moo) | Discouraged - Do not use |
| You | = | Engkau | (En-kow) | Old fashioned, rarely used |
| **You (sir)** | = | **PAK** | (Puck) | Respectful, to adult men |
| **You (madam)** | = | **IBU** | (Ee-boo) | Respectful, to adult women |
| He | = | Dia | (Dee-ah) | The same for men or women |
| She | = | Dia | (Dee-ah) | |
| We | = | Kami | (Kah-mee) | Excludes person spoken to |
| We | = | Kita | (Kee-tah) | Includes person spoken to |
| They/Them | = | Mereka | (M'reck-ah) | |
| Sir (Indonesian) | = | Pak | (Puck) | Respectful, for Indonesians |
| Sir (foreigner) | = | Tuan | (Twahn) | Formal, for foreigners |
| Madam | = | Ibu ('Bu) | (Ee-boo) | Most used, respectful |
| Madam | = | Nyonya | (Nyon-nya) | Less used, more formal |
| Miss | = | Nona | (Non-ah) | |

The respectful custom in Indonesia is to always address elder men as Bapak (or Pak) and elder women as Ibu (or 'Bu). Pak literally means "father" and Ibu literally means "mother" but are used more to denote "sir" or "ma'am". These terms are regularly used as substitutes for other forms of "you" (such as "anda"), being regarded as more respectful. Rather than asking a man "Would you like a drink?" it is more common to say "Would Pak like a drink?" and rather than ask a woman "Where are you going" it is more common to say "Where is Ibu going?"

Local languages in the two most visited islands vary greatly from basic Indonesian, and although the Indonesian terms are totally acceptable, sometimes by using the local pronouns you will get a better reaction because you've bothered to learn a few of their local words. Try using these words and watch the local's faces light up with joy! There are 3 levels of Balinese language, so try to learn the "High Balinese" as it is considered more polite.

# BALINESE

| | | | | |
|---|---|---|---|---|
| Sir | = | Pa | (Paw) | To men old enough to be a father |
| Older Brother | = | Beli | (Blee) | To "older brother" aged men |
| Younger Brother | = | Gus | (Goos) | To "younger brother" aged men, boys |
| Ma'am | = | Me | (May) | To women old enough to be a mother |
| Miss | = | m'Bok | (m'Bok) | To "older sister" aged women |
| Miss | = | Geg | (Gek) | To young girls, teenagers |
| **Thank You** | = | **Matur sukseme** | **(Mah-tour sook-sah-moor)** | |

# JAVANESE

| | | | | |
|---|---|---|---|---|
| Sir | = | Pak | (Puck) | To all "fatherly" men |
| Brother ("Mate") | = | Mas | (Mus) | To all "brotherly" men |
| Miss | = | mBak | (m'Buck) | To all "sisterly" women |
| Thank You | = | Matur Nuwun | (Mah-tour Noo-woon) | |

With all this information, it could be easy to become confused. If you do, just remember to call all women **IBU** and all men **PAK**. It's always better to be overly respectful than the reverse.

# FAMILY & RELATIONSHIPS

| | | | |
|---|---|---|---|
| Wife | = | Isteri | (Is-t'ree) |
| Husband | = | Suami | (Swah-mee) |
| Mother | = | Ibu | (Ee-boo) |
| Father | = | Bapak or Pak or Ayah | (Bah-Puck/ Puck/ Aye-ah) |
| Grandmother | = | Nenek | (Neh-neck) |
| Grandfather | = | Kakek | (Kah-keck) |
| | | | |
| Child | = | Anak | (Ah-nuck) |
| Daughter | = | Anak perempuan | (Ah-nuck purr-om-pwahn) |
| Son | = | Anak laki | (Ah-nuck lucky) |
| Older sister | = | Kakak | (Kah-kahk) |
| Older brother | = | Abang | (Ah-bahng) |
| Younger sibling | = | Adik | (Ah-dick) |
| | | | |
| Aunt | = | Bibi | (Bee-bee) |
| Uncle | = | Paman or Om | (Pah-mahn/ Om) |
| Niece/Nephew | = | Keponakan | (K'paw-Nahk-ahn) |
| Cousin | = | Misan | (Mee-sahn) |
| | | | |
| Relative | = | Famili | (Fah-mi-lee) |
| Family | = | Keluarga | (K'loo-Ah-ga) |
| Mother-in-law | = | Ibu mertua | (Ee-boo m'rr-Too-ah) |
| Father-in-law | = | Ayah mertua | (AYE-ah m'rr-Too-ah) |
| | | | |
| Friend | = | Kawan | (Kah-wahn) |
| Lover | = | Kekasih | (K'Kah-see) |
| Sweetheart | = | Pacar | (Pah-charr) |
| Fiance | = | Tunangan | (Too-nahng-ahn) |
| Married | = | Nikah | (Nik-ah) |
| Divorced | = | Cerai | (Ch-Rye) |
| Bachelor | = | Bujang | (Boo-jahng) |
| Widow | = | Janda | (Jahn-da) |

# QUESTIONS

| | | | |
|---|---|---|---|
| What? | = | Apa? | (Up-ah) |
| Who? | = | Siapa? | (See-up-ah) |
| | | | |
| **When?** | = | Kapan? | (Kah-pahn) |
| When... (**\*Not** a question) | = | Waktu | (Wahk-too) |
| Where? (at a place) | = | Dimana? | (Dee-mah-nah) or "Mana?" |
| To Where? (direction) | = | Kemana? | (K'Mah-nah) |
| | | | |
| Why? | = | Kenapa? | (K'Nahp-ah) or... |
| Why? | = | Mengapa? | (M'ng-up-ah) |
| | | | |
| How? | = | Bagaimana? | (Bug-eye-mah-nah) |
| How many? | = | Berapa? | (Burr-ah-pah) |
| How much is this? | = | Berapa ini? | (Burr-ah-pah in-ee) |
| How much money? | = | Berapa uang? | (Burr-ah-pah wahng) |
| How long? (time) | = | Berapa lama? | (Burr-ah-pah lah-mah) |
| How far? | = | Berapa jauh? | (Burr-ah-pah Jow-Ooh) |
| How old? (age) | = | Berapa umur? | (Burr-ah-pah oom-oor) |
| | | | |
| Which one? | = | Yang mana? | (Young mah-nah) |
| What time....? | = | Jam berapa? | (Jahm burr-ah-pah) |
| Which bus ....? | = | Bis yang mana? | (Bis young-mah-nah) |

# APAKAH

Apakah (Up-ah-kah) is a multi purpose word for whenever you want to ask a question. Place it at the start of any sentence and it turns a statement into a question. Use it wherever you would use "Do?","Can?", "Will?", "Does?", "Is?".

| | | |
|---|---|---|
| DO you want to eat now? | = | APAKAH anda mau makan sekarang? |
| CAN I borrow your car?" | = | APAKAH saya bisa pinjam mobil anda? |
| WILL you wait here?" | = | APAKAH anda akan tunggu disini? |
| DOES the car have petrol?" | = | APAKAH mobil ada benzin? |
| IS he joining us?" | = | APAKAH dia ikut kami? |

# BALI NAMES

Most Balinese village people belong to the Sudra Caste and share four names, whether male or female.

The first born is named **Wayan** (Why-ahn)
The second born is named **Made** (Mah-day)
The third born is named **Nyoman** (Nyo-mahn)
The fourth born is named **Ketut** (K-Toot) (like "foot")

The fifth born repeats Wayan, sixth repeats Made and so on.

Higher castes have titles. **Agung** (Ah-goong) for males and females of the Kesatria royal caste. Ida Ayu (Ee-dah Eye-You) or **Dayu** (Die-You) for females and **Ida Bagus** (Ee-dah Bah-goos) for males of the priestly Brahmana caste.

They also have unique personal names such as heroes and heroines of the Hindu religion, in the same way we have Christian names. There are 3 different Balinese languages, low, medium and high. Indonesian is taught at school.

# PARDON ME?

Chances are, the first time you try speaking Indonesian to a local you will not understand all the words in their reply. You might understand the main idea of their sentence, but not a lot of the in-between words. Here are some handy phrases to explain you are still just learning, and asking for them to help you understand more fully.

| | | |
|---|---|---|
| Sorry, I don't understand | = | Ma'af, saya tidak mengerti. (Mah-Uff sigh-ah tee-duck m'ng-err-tee) |
| I speak only a little Indonesian | = | Saya bicara sedikit saja "Bahasa Indonesia" (Sigh-ah bee-chah-rra s'dee-kit sah-ja Ba-hah-sa Indo-nay-see-ah) |
| Please speak slowly | = | Tolong bicara pelan-pelan. (Toe-long bee-chah-rra p'lahn p'lahn) |
| Please repeat again slowly | = | Tolong ulang lagi pelan-pelan (Toe-long oo-lung lah-gee p'lahn p'lahn) |
| Please write (it) | = | Tolong tulis (Toe-long too-lis) |
| What is the meaning of (word)? | = | Apa arti (word)? (Up-ah ahrr-tee) word? |

These indispensable sentences are greatly enhanced by saying "Sorry sir/ma'am" prior to each sentence - "**Ma'af Pak**" or "**Ma'af Ibu**" depending upon whom you are addressing. Even though you are saying you have not yet fully learnt their language, your manners will show you have already learnt how to show respect.

The Indonesian locals will readily help you learn more of their language, and you will find they are The Best Teachers of all! Don't be afraid to make mistakes - they are a necessary part of any learning experience. The more you politely ask the locals to help you, the easier learning Indonesian will become.

If the lessons in this book seem a little daunting right now, don't worry - you will learn more in one week in Indonesia than 3 months at home with a book! So reserve that airline ticket now!

# HELP - I'M SICK!

**Please help, I'm sick.**          Minta tolong, saya sakit.     (**Min-tah toe-long sigh-ah suck-kit**)
Please call a doctor to here     Tolong panggil doktor kesini
Please take me to a hospital     Tolong antar saya ke rumah sakit.

| | | | |
|---|---|---|---|
| Doctor | - Dokter | Hospital | - Rumah sakit |
| Cut | - Luka | Infection | - Infeksi |
| Broken bone | - Patah tulang | Diarrhoea | - Menceret |
| Fever | - Deman | Vomit | - Muntah |
| Sprain | - Keseleo | Stomach upset | - Sakit perut |
| Toothache | - Sakit gigi | A cold | - Pilek |
| Flu | - Flu | Medicine | - Obat |
| Antibiotic | - Antibiotik | Headache | - Sakit kepala |
| Pharmacy | - Apotik | Stitch | - Jahit |

**Thanks for your help!**   -   **Terima kasih atas pertolongan anda.**

# USEFUL EVERYDAY WORDS

| | | | |
|---|---|---|---|
| Yes | Ya | Because | Karena |
| No | Tidak | Perhaps/Maybe | Mungkin/Barangkali |
| Here | Disini | About (concerning) | Tentang |
| There | Disana | About (approximately) | Kira-kira |
| (and) Then | Kemudian or Lalu | Similar to | Seperti |
| | | | |
| Many/Lots of | Banyak | Big | Besar |
| Very many | Banyak-banyak | Small | Kecil |
| An awful lot | Banyak sekali | A little | Sedikit |
| | | | |
| And | Dan | Old (person) | Tua |
| But | Tetapi/Tapi | Old (thing) | Lama |
| If | Kalau | Young | Muda |
| At | Di | New | Baru |
| | | | |
| Or | Atau | Beautiful (person) | Cantik |
| With | Dengan | Beautiful (view) | Indah |
| | | | |
| This | Ini | Delicious | Enak/ Sedap |
| That | Itu | Cheap | Murah |
| Like this | Begini | Expensive | Mahal |
| Like that | Begitu | Hungry | Lapar |
| | | | |
| More | Lebih | Thirsty | Haus |
| Less | Kurang | Toilet | Kamar kecil |
| Wait | Tunggu | Toilet | W.C. (Way-Say) |
| | | | |
| Love | Cinta | Sick/Sore | Sakit |
| Beforehand | Dulu | Like | Suka |
| Shy | Malu | Embarrassed | Malu |

# WEATHER

| | | | |
|---|---|---|---|
| Hot | Panas | Cold | Dingin |
| Wind | Angin | Rain | Hujan |
| Sun | Mata hari | Sunshine | Sinar mata hari |
| Strong Wind | Angin Keras | Cloudy | Mendung |
| Sunrise | Mata hari terbit | Sunset | Mata hari terbenam |
| Moon | Bulan | Full moon | Bulan purnama |
| Humid | Lembab | Rainbow | Pelangi |

# COLOURS

| | | | |
|---|---|---|---|
| Black | Hitam | White | Putih |
| Gold | Mas | Silver | Perak |
| Red | Merah | Blue | Biru |
| Yellow | Kuning | Green | Hijau |
| Purple | Unggu | Brown | Coklat |
| Light | Muda | Dark | Tua |

# NUMBERS

| TEENS | = BELAS | (Blahs) | | TENS | = PULUH | (Poo-looH) |
|---|---|---|---|---|---|---|
| HUNDREDS | = RATUS | (Rrah-toos) | | THOUSANDS | = RIBU | (Rree-boo) |
| MILLIONS | = JUTA | (Joo-ta) | | | | |

| 0 | = Nol | (Nol) | | | |
|---|---|---|---|---|---|
| 1 | = Satu | (Sah-too) | 21 | = | Dua Puluh Satu |
| 2 | = Dua | (Doo-ah) | 22 | = | Dua Puluh Dua |
| 3 | = Tiga | (Tee-gah) | 23 | = | Dua Puluh Tiga |
| 4 | = Empat | (Um-putt) | 24 | = | Dua Puluh Empat |
| 5 | = Lima | (Lee-ma) | 25 | = | Dua Puluh Lima |
| 6 | = Enam | (e-Num) | 26 | = | Dua Puluh Enam |
| 7 | = Tujuh | (Too-joo) | 27 | = | Dua Puluh Tujuh |
| 8 | = Delapan | (D'Lup-un) | 28 | = | Dua Puluh Delapan |
| 9 | = Sembilan | (Sem-bee-lun) | 29 | = | Dua Puluh Sembilan |
| 10 | = Sepuluh | (S'Poo-looh) | 30 | = | Tiga Puluh |
| 11 | = Sebelas | (S'B'Lahs) | 40 | = | Empat Puluh |
| 12 | = Dua Belas | (Doo-ah B'Lahs) | 50 | = | Lima Puluh |
| 13 | = Tiga Belas | (Tee-ga B'Lahs) | 60 | = | Enam Puluh |
| 14 | = Empat Belas | (uM-Putt B'Lahs) | 70 | = | Tujuh Puluh |
| 15 | = Lima Belas | (Lee-ma B'Lahs) | 80 | = | Delapan Puluh |
| 16 | = Enam Belas | (e-Num B'Lahs) | 90 | = | Sembilan Puluh |
| 17 | = Tujuh Belas | (Too-joo B'Lahs) | 100 | = | Seratus (S'Rahtoos) |
| 18 | = Delapan Belas | (D'Lup-un B'Lahs) | 250 | = | Dua Ratus Lima Puluh |
| 19 | = Sembilan Belas | (Sem-bee-lun B'Lahs) | 500 | = | Lima Ratus |
| 20 | = Dua Puluh | (Doo-ah Poo-looh) | 1000 | = | Seribu (S'Ree-boo) |

| Half | = Setengah | (S'Teng-ah) | 1,000,000 | = Se Juta (Sir Joota) |
|---|---|---|---|---|
| Quarter | = Seperempat | (S'P'rem-paht) | 2,500,000 | = Dua Juta Lima Ratus Ribu |
| Plus | = Tambah | Minus = Kurang | Times = Kali | Divided by = Dibagi |

# BLACK MAGIC

Black Magic is believed in all over Indonesia. It is nothing for the average traveller to worry about, but surfers need to understand one local legend about **The Queen of the Southern Seas** (Ratu Nyai Loro Kidul).

The open ocean power in Indonesia is quite awesome, with ground-swells travelling all the way from Antarctica. Many drownings occur at remote beaches, especially along the wild southern shores of Java. For generations Javanese spiritual mystics have attributed these drownings to the desire of The Queen of the Southern Seas for handsome young men. Every year this ocean spirit reportedly plucks several men from the beaches to be her lovers under the sea, and it is said they are always wearing **green shorts.**

Naturally, anyone who believes in this centuries-old superstition will never wear green shorts into the ocean. Most surfers who regularly visit Indonesia leave their green shorts at home. Local surfers never risk it. At least one surfer has died at Uluwatu while supposedly wearing green shorts. He was Bob Laverty, one of the first group of 8 surfers to surf Grajagan in 1972. He was surfing **Uluwatu** shortly after discovering G-Land, when his body was mysteriously found washed up on the shore. As he was carried across the reef, a sea snake wrapped itself around his body.

Many mystic occurrences are attributed to The Queen of the Southern Seas, from drownings, to tsunamis, to thousands of fish washing up on the shore which happens in October each year. To prevent disasters, many locals make regular offerings to placate her. Rice, flowers and incense are placed on the sand in prayer, with occasional animal blood sacrifices. The Samudra Hotel at **Pelabuhan Ratu** (Harbour of the Queen) in West Java has a room permanently left empty for her. This was decided necessary after a tidal wave washed-out their opening ceremony in 1966, despite warnings from an old local shaman to make offerings to her first. In 1991 the Hotel Bali Beach in Sanur caught fire, with 95% of the hotel destroyed. Only one room remained untouched by the flames - it was room 327, the one left empty for Ratu Nyai Loro Kidul. **The Grand Bali Beach Hotel** has now been rebuilt, with her room even more luxuriously decorated. Bali Hindu priests make offerings and prayers every day in the hotel grounds.

# USEFUL VERBS

Although Formal Indonesian adds several Prefixes (such as mem-, meng- and ber-) before the root verb, this is very complex, and thus, in a typical Indonesian fashion, the majority of the locals dispense with them for most everyday conversations, and you too will be understood using just the root verb. (Learn the prefixes next year OK?)

| | | | |
|---|---|---|---|
| Ask for | Minta | Ask of someone | Tanya |
| Arrive | Tiba | | |
| | | | |
| Bring | Bawa | Buy | Beli |
| Be/Exist | Ada | Begin | Mulai |
| Bargain (to..) | Tawar | | |
| | | | |
| Can (able) | Dapat | Can (possible) | Bisa |
| Can (permission) | Boleh | Close | Tutup |
| Carry | Angkat | | |
| | | | |
| Drive/Sightsee | Melancong | Dance | Tari |
| Drink | Minum | Eat | Makan |
| | | | |
| Fly | Terbang | Forget | Lupa |
| Finish | Selesai | Give | Kasih |
| Go | Pergi | Go home | Pulang |
| Get | Dapat | | |
| | | | |
| Have (present) | Ada | Have (own) | Punya |
| Hear | Dengar | Inform | Beritahu |
| | | | |
| Know | Tahu | Kiss | Cium (chee-oom) |
| Laugh | Ketawa | Leave | Barangkat |
| | | | |
| Make | Buat/Bikin | Meet | Ketemu |
| Misunderstand | Salah faham | Need | Perlu |
| | | | |
| Open | Buka | | |
| | | | |
| Paint | Lukis | Pay | Bayar |
| Play | Main | Run | Lari |
| Remember | Ingat | Return | Kembali |
| Return home | Pulang | Receive | Terima |
| | | | |
| See | Lihat | Sport/exercise | Olah raga |
| Sell | Jual | Sit | Duduk |
| Stand | Berdiri | Smell | Cium |
| Sing | Nyanyi | Swim | Berenang |
| Show | Lihatkan | Sleep | Tidur |
| Send | Kirim | | |
| | | | |
| Talk | Bicara | Tell/Say/Speak | Berkata |
| Think | Pikir | There is/are | Ada |
| There will be | Ada | There is not | Tidak ada |
| Take | Ambil | | |
| | | | |
| Understand | Mengerti | Wake/get up | Bangun |
| Want | Mau | Walk/Go/Travel | Jalan |
| Wish for | Ingin | Wash (clothes) | Cuci |
| Wash (person) | Mandi | Work | Kerja |
| Write | Tulis | | |

# FOOD

Nasi Padang, hot and spicy. Photo: Nate Lawrence

| | | | |
|---|---|---|---|
| Apple | = Apel | Fried rice | = Nasi Goreng |
| Breakfast | = Makan pagi | Fried Noodles | = Mie goreng |
| Bread | = Roti | Fruit | = Buah |
| Butter | = Butter | Fork | = Garpu |
| Banana | = Pisang | Fish | = Ikan |
| Boiled | = Rebus | Fried egg | = Telor goreng |
| Boiled water | = Air rebus | Glass | = Gelas |
| Beer | = Bir | Goat | = Kambing |
| Beef | = Sapi | Hot (spicy) | = Pedas |
| Boiled egg | = Telor rebus | Hot (temperature) | = Panas |
| Bitter | = Pahit | Hot tea | = Teh panas |
| Cafe | = Rumah makan | Ice | = Es |
| Coconut | = Kelapa | Iced water | = Air es |
| Cold | = Dingin | Iced tea | = Es Teh |
| Cake | = Kue | Knife | = Pisau |
| Coffee | = Kopi | Lunch | = Makan siang |
| Cordial | = Stroop | Lemon | = Limon |
| Chilli | = Lombok | Lime | = Jeruk nipis |
| Chilli sauce | = Sambal | Lamb | = Domba |
| Cup | = Cangkir | Lobster | = Udang besar |
| Chicken | = Ayam | Liver | = Hati |
| Dining room | = Kamar makan | Margarine | = Mentega |
| **Drink** | **= Minuman** | Mango | = Mangga |
| Dinner | = Makan malam | Milk | = Susu |
| Delicious | = Enak | More please | = Minta tambah |
| Dumpling | = Pangsit | Noodles | = Mie |
| Egg | = Telor | Orange | = Jeruk |
| **Food** | **= Makanan** | Orange juice | = Air jeruk |

| | | | |
|---|---|---|---|
| Pork | = Babi | | |
| Prawns | = Udang | | |
| Pepper | = Merica | | |
| Plate | = Piring | | |
| Pineapple | = Nanas | | |
| Restaurant | = Restoran | | |
| Roadside kiosk | – Warung | | |
| Rice (cooked) | = Nasi | | |
| Rice (uncooked) | = Beras | | |
| Rice (in field) | = Padi | | |
| Soup | = Soto/Kuah | | |
| Sauce | = Saus/Kuah | | |
| Special | = Istimewa | | |
| Spoon | = Sendok | | |
| Sweet | = Manis | | |
| Sugar | = Gula | | |
| Salt | = Garam | | |
| Soya sauce | = Kecap | | |
| Salty | = Asin | | |
| Sweet soya sauce | = Kecap manis | | |
| Sour | = Asam | | |
| Tomato sauce | = Saus tomat | | |
| Tea | = Teh | | |
| Tasty | = Sedap | | |
| Vegetables | = Sayur | | |
| Vinegar | = Cuka | | |
| **Water** | **= Air** | | |

| | |
|---|---|
| **Please may I have** | **= Minta** |
| Please eat! (Bon Apetit!) | = Selamat makan! |
| Thank you, it was delicious! | = Terima kasih, enak sekali |

# A TYPICAL BASIC CONVERSATION

Here is a typical conversation with some of the questions you will encounter most every day - "What's your name?", "Where are you from?" etc  This example is between a male tourist ■ and a hotel housemaid □

| english | indonesian | pronunciation |
|---|---|---|
| ■ Good morning ma'am. How are you? | Selamat pagi ibu. Apa kabar? | S'lah-maht pah-gee ee-boo. Up-ah kah-barr? |
| □ Good morning sir. I'm well. | Selamat pagi tuan. Kabar baik. | S'lah-maht pah-gee too-ahn. Kah-barr bike. |
| Sir can speak Indonesian? | Tuan bisa bicara bahasa Indonesia? | Too-ahn bee-sa bee-charr-ah ba-ha-sa Indo-nay-see-ah? |
| ■ Not yet ma'am. Just a little. I'm still learning. | Belum ibu. Sedikit saja. Saya masih belajar. | B'loom ee-boo. S'dee-kit sah-ja. Sigh-ah mah-see b'ludj-arr. |
| □ Sir is from where? | Tuan dari mana? | Too-ahn dah-ree mah-na? |
| ■ I'm from Australia. | Saya dari Australie. | Sigh-ah dah-ree  Os-trah-lee. |
| □ Australia where? | Australie mana? | Os-trah-lee mah-na? |
| ■ Sydney | Sydney | Sydney |
| □ Good. Many people from Sydney come here. | Bagus! Banyak orang dari Sydney datang kesini. | Bah-goos! Bun-yuk or-rung dah-ree Sydney dah-tongue ke-sin-ee. |
| ■ What's (your) name  ma'am? | Siapa nama ibu? | See-up-ah nah-ma  ee-boo? |
| □ My name's Wayan Sari. What's (your) name sir? | Nama saya Wayan Sari. Siapa nama tuan? | Nah-ma sigh-ah Why-ahn Sah-ree. See-up-ah nah-ma too-ahn? |
| ■  My name's Bob. | Nama saya Bob. | Nah-ma sigh-ah Bob. |
| □ Bob who? | Bob siapa? | Bob see-up-ah? |
| ■  Bob Smith. | Bob Smith. | Bob Smith. |
| □ I'm pleased to meet you. | Saya senang ketemu anda. | Sigh-ah s'nang k'temoo ahn-da. |
| ■  (I feel the) same  Mrs. Wayan | Sama-sama Ibu Wayan. | Sum-ah sum-ah ee-boo Why-ahn |
| □ Does Mr Bob have a wife? | Apakah Tuan Bob punya istri? | Up-ah-kah too-ahn Bob poon-ya is-tree? |
| ■ Yes. | Ya. | Yah. |
| □ Bob has children? | Bob punya anak-anak? | Bob poon-ya ah-nuck ah-nuck? |
| ■  Yes, (I) have. | Ya, punya. | Yah, poon-ya. |
| □ How many children? | Berapa anak-anak? | B'rah-pa ah-nuck ah-nuck? |
| ■  Only one.  A boy. | Hanya satu. Anak laki. | Hun-ya sah-too. Ah-nuck lucky. |
| □ I have two girls. | Saya punya dua perempuan. | Sigh-ah poon-ya doo-ah p'rom-pwahn. |

94

| English | Indonesian | Pronunciation |
|---|---|---|
| ■ How old? | Berapa umur? | B'rah-pa oo-moor? |
| □ The big one is age ten.<br>The small one is age five years.<br>Where is your wife now? | Yang besar umur sepuluh.<br>Yang kecil umur lima tahun .<br>Dimana istri tuan sekarang? | Young b'sarr oo-moor s'poo-looh.<br>Young k'chill oo-moor lee-ma town.<br>Dee-mah-na is-tree too-ahn s'kar-rung? |
| ■ My wife is at the shop.<br>My son is at the beach. | Istri saya di toko.<br>Anak laki saya di pantai. | Is-tree sigh-ah dee toe-koe.<br>Ah-nuck lucky sigh-ah dee pun-tie. |
| □ Bob's child likes surfing? | Anak Bob suka main ski? | Ah-nuck Bob sue-ka mine-skee? |
| ■ Likes it! Every day! | Suka! Setiap hari! | Sue-ka! S'tee-up ha-ree! |
| □ How long (will) Bob stay here? | Berapa lama Bob tinggal disini? | B'rah-pa lah-ma Bob ting-gahl dis-in-ee? |
| ■ Only three days. | Hanya tiga hari. | Hun-ya tee-ga ha-ree. |
| □ That's a shame.<br>Not long. | Kasihan.<br>Tidak lama. | Kah-see-hahn.<br>Tee-duck lah-ma. |
| ■ But I'll return in six days | Tetapi saya kembali di enam hari. | T'tupee sigh-ah k'm-bali de e'num haree |
| □ Great!<br>Hopefully we<br>(will/can) meet again. | Baik!<br>Mudah-mudahan kita<br>(akan/bisa) ketemu lagi. | Bike!<br>Moo-dah moo-dah-hahn keeta<br>(ah-kahn/bee-sa) k'temoo lah-gee. |
| ■ Hopefully.<br>I like practicing<br>Indonesian with you. | Mudah-mudahan.<br>Saya senang praktek<br>Bahasa Indonesia sama anda. | Moo-dah moo-dah-hahn.<br>Sigh-ah s'nung pruck-tek<br>Ba-ha-sa Indo-nay-see-ah sum-a ahn-da |
| □ Sir speaks<br>Indonesian very well. | Tuan bicara Bahasa<br>Indonesia bagus sekali. | Too-ahn bee-chah-ra Ba-ha-sa<br>Indo-nay-see-ah bah-goos s'kah-lee. |
| ■ Thank you ma'am. | Terima kasih ibu. | T'ree-ma kah-see ee-boo. |
| □ Same (to you).<br>Excuse me, Mr Bob.<br>I must work again. | Sama-sama.<br>Permisi Tuan Bob.<br>Saya harus kerja lagi. | Sum-ah sum-ah.<br>Purr-miss-ee too-ahn Bob.<br>Sigh-ah har-roos kerr-ja lah-gee. |
| ■ Of course Mrs Wayan.<br>Please.<br>Thanks again. | Tentu saja Ibu Wayan.<br>Silahkan.<br>Terima kasih lagi. | Ten-too sah-ja Ee-boo Why-ahn.<br>Sil-ah-kahn.<br>T'ree-ma kah-see lah-gee. |
| □ Until we meet again. | Sampai kita ketemu/<br>jumpa lagi. | Sum-pie kee-ta k'temoo/<br>joom-pah lah-gee. |
| ■ Maybe we meet<br>tomorrow morning? | Mungkin kita ketemu<br>besok pagi? | Moong-kin keeta k'temoo<br>bay-sock pah-gee? |
| □ Yes. Good bye. | Ya. Selamat tinggal. | Yah. S'lah-maht ting-gahl. |
| ■ Good bye. | Selamat jalan. | S'lah-mut jah-lahn. |

Create your own simple conversation like the one on these pages. Write your questions and answers in English, then translate it to Indonesian, looking up new words in your dictionary ("kamus"). This way you will make the most of your time by learning only exactly what you want to learn, nothing more or less. Record yourself saying the words so you can listen back to check up on your pronunciation.

A broad Aussie accent is without doubt the most common problem most beginners have. It is essential you mimick the pronunciation and accent of the Indonesian people, in the same way you would do to speak French or Italian with the correct accent. The best way to prepare the groundwork for a good accent it to learn the distinctive sounds of the Indonesian alphabet, especially the vowels A,E,I,O,U. Practice reciting them until it is second nature to you.

# TIME

| | | | | | | |
|---|---|---|---|---|---|---|
| Second | = | Detik | | Minute | = | Menit |
| Hour | = | Jam | | Day | = | Hari |
| Week | = | Minggu | | Month | = | Bulan |
| Year | = | Tahun | | | | |

| | | | | |
|---|---|---|---|---|
| 1 o'clock | = | Jam satu | | "Hour one" |
| 7:20 pm | = | Jam tujuh duapuluh malam | | "Hour Seven: Twenty night" |
| To (the hour) | = | Kurang (less) | | eg 5 to 7 o'clock = Jam tujuh kurang lima |
| Past (the hour) | = | Lewat | | eg 5 past 7 = Jam tujuh lewat lima |
| **Half (to)** | = | Setengah | | eg Half past 7 = Setengah delapan (**Half to** 8) |

*In Indonesian, time is always stated as **Half TO** rather than "Half past"

| | | | | |
|---|---|---|---|---|
| What time is it? | = | Jam berapa? | | Pronounced "Jahm Burr-up-ah?" = What hour? |
| Six o'clock AM | = | Jam enam pagi | | "Jahm en-num pah-gee" = Hour six morning |
| Six o'clock PM | = | Jam enam malam | | "Jahm en-num mah-lahm" = Hour six night |
| 12 o'clock noon | = | Jam duabelas siang | | (Siang = 11am - 3pm approximately) |
| 12 o'clock night | = | Jam duabelas malam | | (Malam = after sunset) |
| 4 o'clock pm | = | Jam empat sore | | (Sore = after 3 pm but before sunset) |

| | | | | | | |
|---|---|---|---|---|---|---|
| Today | = | Hari ini | | Tomorrow | = | Besok |
| Night | = | Malam | | Tonight | = | Malam ini |
| Yesterday | = | Kemarin | | This week | = | Minggu ini |

| | | | | | | |
|---|---|---|---|---|---|---|
| Morning | = | Pagi (Sunrise-11 am) | | Next week | = | Minggu depan |
| Mid day | = | Siang (11 am-3 pm) | | Last week | = | Minggu lalu |
| Afternoon | = | Sore (3 pm-sunset) | | Just now | = | Baru saja |

| | | | | | | |
|---|---|---|---|---|---|---|
| Last night | = | Tadi malam | | When? | = | Kapan? |
| This morning | = | Tadi pagi | | Later | = | Nanti |
| Last Monday | = | Hari senin lalu | | In a moment | = | Sebentar |
| Next Monday | = | Hari senin depan | | Soon | = | Sebentar lagi |

| | | | | | | |
|---|---|---|---|---|---|---|
| One year ago | = | Satu tahun yang lalu | | Next year | = | Tahun depan |
| 3 more years | = | Tiga tahun lagi | | Not yet | = | Belum |

| | | | | | | |
|---|---|---|---|---|---|---|
| Now | = | Sekarang | | Patience | = | Sabar |
| Quickly | = | Cepat | | Let's go! | = | Mari |
| Before | = | Sebelum | | Let's go! | = | Ayo (slang) |
| After | = | Sesudah/Setelah | | Immediately | = | Segera |

**Rubber Time:** Indonesians have a relaxed attitude to time. Unlike the typical fast living western city worker known as a "clock watcher", their predominantly rural society is more attuned to longer frames of time, "weather watchers". Hence the extra time zone "siang" which denotes the hottest hours in the middle of the day from 11 to 3.
NB. If you ask someone "What time will the bus leave" they may not be sure of the exact hour. So they will tell you what they think you want to hear: "Soon" or "Not long". No-one is in too much of a hurry anyway, because it's so hot.

| | | | | | | |
|---|---|---|---|---|---|---|
| Rubber time | = | Jam karet | | Some time later | = | Besok-besok |
| Whenever | = | Kapan saja | | Just relax | = | Tenang saja |

| | | |
|---|---|---|
| Monday | = | Hari Senin |
| Tuesday | = | Hari Selasa |
| Wednesday | = | Hari Rabuh |
| Thursday | = | Hari Kamis |
| Friday | = | Hari Juma'at |
| Saturday | = | Hari Sabtu |
| Sunday | = | Hari Minggu |

# ON THE ROAD

Indonesia's roads can lead to adventure and good times, but they can also lead to an abrupt accidental end to your holiday. The roads can be extremely crowded, pot-holed and dangerous. See our **Transport Tips** later in the book. On the next page are some handy words and sentences that may come in handy on your Road to Adventure.

**"Travel is fatal to prejudice, bigotry, and narrow-mindedness." Mark Twain**

Lombok Fish transport

Ubud kids, 1975

Suroto, Java 1982

Lake Batur 1975

Sumatra bridge crossing

Nusa Dua, 1977

G-Land taxi

Mr Perama Tours, 1977

Denpasar horse carts, 1975

# on the road - helpful words

| | |
|---|---|
| Please go slowly & carefully. | Harap pelan dan hati-hati. |
| Please go slower. | Mohon lebih pelan. |
| Don't go fast! | Jangan cepat! |
| Don't overtake! | Jangan salip! |
| Just go slowly. | Pelan-pelan saja. |
| Look out! | Awas! (Ah-wahs) |
| If you don't go slowly... I will not pay. | Kalau anda tidak pelan... Saya tidak bayar. |

| | |
|---|---|
| I want to rent a car. | Saya mau sewa mobil. |
| Where can I rent a car? | Dimana saya bisa sewa mobil? |
| Where can I buy petrol? | Dimana saya bisa beli bensin? |
| Where is a mechanic? | Dimana bengkel? |
| Where is a tyre repairer? | Dimana pres ban? |
| Please check | Tolong periksa |

| Please check | | Tolong periksa | |
|---|---|---|---|
| | - the brakes. | | - rem. |
| | - the oil. | | - minyak. |
| | - the water. | | - air. |
| | - the air. | | - angin. |

| | | | |
|---|---|---|---|
| Motorbike | - Sepeda motor | Car | - Mobil |
| Push bike | - Sepeda (S'Pay-da) | Minibus | - Colt |
| Bus | - Bis | Minibus | - Bemo ("Bay-moh") |
| Taxi | - Taksi | Train | - Kereta api |
| Truck | - Truk | Boat | - Kapal laut |

| | | | |
|---|---|---|---|
| Sail boat | - Kapal layar | Outrigger | - Perahu ("Prr-ow-oo") |
| Aeroplane | - Pesawat | Helicopter | - Helikopter |

| | | | |
|---|---|---|---|
| Left | - Kiri | Right | - Kanan |
| Continue | - Terus | Stop | - Berhenti |
| Reverse | - Mundur | Turn | - Belok |

| | | | |
|---|---|---|---|
| Petrol station | - Pompa bensin | Dead end | - Jalan buntu |
| Air conditioning | - A.C. (Ah Say) | Rough road | - Jalan rusak |
| Flat tyre | - Ban kempes | Insurance | - Assuransi |
| Accident | - Kecelakaan | Please help | - Minta tolong |

| | |
|---|---|
| Please call a mechanic here | - Tolong panggil bengkel kesini. |
| This car is broken down | - Mobil ini rusak. |
| Please change the car | - Minta ganti mobil. |
| **Sorry, I will pay for repairs** | **- Ma'af.  Saya bayar perbaikan.** |

# SHOPPING

## the art of friendly bargaining

Indonesia now has excellent modern supermarkets in most major cities and tourist resorts, with fixed prices often cheaper than street-side hawkers. Smaller shops and market stalls do not feature price labels which usually indicates that the price is open to negotiation.

Most tourist souvenir items are negotiable, and you are expected to enter into friendly bargaining sessions to strike a deal that suits both parties. The final price depends upon lots of things, not just the tourist's ability to pay a higher price than a local (understandable when you consider that most Indonesians earn less than $25 a week).

Bargaining is an old Indonesian institution. There have always been different prices for different people. The lowest price is for family and people from the same village, slightly more for people from other villages, even more for people from other Indonesian islands and then top price for foreigners. Australians often get charged less than Americans or Japanese. Enter into the fun of it, and you will enjoy bargaining.

If you intend buying more than just one item, let the seller know, as this is of major consideration. Also very important is the friendly attitude you display during your bargaining session.

The more you smile and joke and gently cajole the seller, the more likely a price reduction can be bargained, but try not to lose sight of how cheap things really are.

Never attempt a stony-faced confrontation, perhaps saying the shop next door is cheaper - you will certainly be told to go there instead!

Shopping first thing in the morning sometimes creates cheaper prices than later in the day, because some sellers consider an early sale as "good luck" for the coming day. Also last thing in the afternoon can create bargains for perishable fresh fruit and vegetables, or even tourist items if the seller has a need for cash right away - to pay rent for example, or even just for a night out at the movies. Restaurants are almost exclusively "fixed price", as are hotels. Smaller home-stay hotels (losmen, penginapan) may give a discount if you stay a week or longer, but this must be negotiated from your first meeting with the owner, prior to moving in. Even big hotels will negotiate. Public transport is mostly fixed price, although "chartering" a vehicle to take just you and your friends directly to your destination will involve some hard bargaining.

Ask other tourists what things generally cost - although you could ask a local, most are embarrassed to give an incorrect price and perhaps disappoint you or create a problem with local sellers - better to ask around among other tourists. Prices can often vary from day to day.

Small roadside kiosks ("Warung") offer local food and drinks very cheaply. Ask first what something costs, but do not attempt to bargain as this would offend.

## a typical shopping conversation

- ■ How much is a Mixed Rice ma'am?
- ☐ Ten thousand rupiah sir.
- ■ Fine, please may I have one.
- ■ *(No) Thank you, maybe later.

Berapa Nasi Campur ibu?
Sepuluh ribu rupiah tuan.
Baik, minta satu.
*Terima kasih, mungkin nanti.

*The polite way to refuse anything offered to you in Indonesia is to just say "**Terima Kasih**" (thank you) with a smile and a shake of the hand or head. (Tree-mah Kah-see). This implies "**NO** thank you".

- ☐ What are you looking for?
- ☐ What do you want?
- ■ (I'm) Looking for a shirt.
- ■ (I) Want a sarong.
- ■ How much is the price of this ma'am?
- ☐ One hundred thousand rupiah sir.
- ■ Gosh, expensive!
- ■ Thanks anyway, I don't want (it).
- ■ May I bargain ma'am?
- ☐ (You) may.
- ☐ Sorry, fixed price.
- ■ How much if I buy two?
- ■ Good, cheap!
- ■ How much discount if I buy this, and this?
- ☐ Up to you.

Cari apa? (Literally: Seeking what?)
Mau apa? (Literally: Want what?)
(Saya) Cari kemeja.
(Saya) Mau sarung.
Berapa harga ini ibu?
Seratus ribu rupiah tuan.
Aduh, mahal!
Terima kasih saja, saya tidak mau.
Boleh saya tawar ibu?
Boleh.
Ma'af, harga pas.
Berapa kalau saya beli dua?
Bagus, murah!
Berapa korting kalau saya beli ini, dan ini?
Terserah.

| | |
|---|---|
| ■ Can the price come down? | Apakah harga bisa turun? |
| □ How much (do you) want to pay? | Berapa (anda) mau bayar? |
| □ Too cheap! Come up! | Terlalu murah! Naik. |
| ■ Too expensive! Come down! | Terlalu mahal! Turun! |

Once you start bargaining for something, you can't just change your mind and say you didn't really like the colour or whatever - once a price has been settled upon, you're obliged to pay up, so don't just bargain for the sake of it. If the starting price seems way too high, just say "**Terima kasih** saja" which implies "**NO** thank you".

| | |
|---|---|
| ■ Just looking. | Lihat-lihat saja. |
| ■ Sorry, (my) money's finished. | Ma'af, uang (saya) habis. |
| ■ Sorry, (I) don't have any money. | Ma'af, (saya) tidak ada uang. |
| ■ Please keep (it) for me. | Tolong simpan untuk saya. |
| ■ I will pay tomorrow morning. | Saya akan bayar besok pagi. |
| ■ **Thankyou for your help.** | **Terima kasih atas pertolongan anda.** |

You can bargain in street stalls, but not major surfshops

Bol, Welcome to Padang. Photo: Damea Dorsey A-Frame

# EXPLORING THE OUTER ISLANDS

Indonesia has become a popular destination for surfers from all over the world, and now that Bali's famous reefs have become crowded, adventurous surfers are travelling to outer islands in search of perfect waves on isolated, palm-fringed beaches. Hopefully this book will help many surfers discover new breaks and make new friends in the thousands of islands between North Sumatra and West Papua.

**Bahasa Indonesia** is spoken in every province of Indonesia, although some of the more remote locals will have had only a small amount of formal education in Indonesian and you may very well speak Indonesian better than they do. Often schoolkids will understand you even if their parents don't. This is where the true adventurer relies upon a big smile, helpful attitude and manners in communicating. Perhaps find time to learn a few words of the local dialect to show respect eg. Sir, Ma'am, Thankyou, Please etc.

**Please remember** that you are an ambassador for every other surfer to follow, so be courteous and respectful of local customs. The outer islands aren't as tolerant as Bali, so always dress neatly, even though it is 35 degrees in the shade. Because most Indonesian islands follow the Islamic faith, keep this in mind and never walk around outer islands in just shorts or bikinis (even on the beach). Always use the right hand for eating or handing things to people, and never touch anyone with the left hand as this denotes disrespect. Don't touch people's heads (with either hand), and don't use your foot to point towards something. There are many other customs you will learn to respect, so be prepared to treat every new day as a fresh learning experience.

If there are no hotels or losmen available, ask to see the head man of the village ("Kepala desa") to ask for help. You may end up sleeping on someone's floor. Or in a Presidential Guesthouse. Either way, it will be the best place available for you, and you should pay a fair price.

Some remote island areas may not have enough food available for you, no matter how much money you have, so read up about where you intend staying. Lonely Planet guidebooks are excellent. In some remote areas it is often better to give your hosts rice, sugar, coffee (or even beetlenut) rather than cash in payment for your accommodation. Don't be stingy because these people really need whatever you can give them in return for their hospitality. There's nothing worse than hearing some stingy traveller's tales about how little he paid a poor peasant.

One of the major realisations many travellers make is that we "westerners" are very lucky to have been born into affluent societies where good food, good health and international travel are just taken for granted. Share your good karma.

Here are a few words and sentences that may help you find a new Indonesian Perfect Point:

Photo Cory Scott

**Please help. Where is the beach?** Minta tolong, di mana pantai? (Min-tah toe-long, dee-mahna pun-tie)

**Is there a coral reef nearby?** Apakah ada karang dekat? (Up-ah-kah ah-da k'rahng d'kut?)

**How far to the beach?** Berapa jauh ke pantai? (B'rr-ah-pa jow k' pun-tie?)

**Where can I hire an outrigger?** Dimana saya bisa sewa perahu? (Dee-mah-na sigh-ah bee-sa say-wa p'rrow)

**I want to hire a boat.** Saya mau sewa kapal laut. (Sigh-ah mah-oo say-wa kah-pahl lout)

**I'm looking for big waves!** Saya cari ombak-ombak besar. (Sigh-ah chah-rree om-buck om-buck b'sahrr)

# USEFUL SURFING WORDS

| | | |
|---|---|---|
| Wave | = Ombak | (Om-buck) |
| Ocean | = Laut | (Lout) |
| Beach | = Pantai | (Pun-tie) |
| Coral reef | = Karang | (K'Rung) |
| Point | = Tanjung | (Tongue-joong) |
| Sand | = Pasir | (Pah-seerr) |
| | | |
| Wind | = Angin | (Ahng-in) |
| Onshore wind | = Angin laut | (Ahng-in lout) |
| Offshore | = Darat | (Dah-raht) |
| | | |
| Surfing | = Berselancar | (Burr-s'lahn-charr) |
| Surfing (slang) | = Main ski | (Mine Skee) |
| | | |
| Swell | = Gelombang | (Ge-Lohm-bahng) |
| Tube | = Lengkung | (L'ng-koong) |
| Peak | = Puncak | (Pun-chuck) |
| | | |
| High tide | = Air pasang | (Air Pah-sahng) |
| Low tide | = Air surut | (Air soo-root) |
| | | |
| Deep water | = Air dalam | (Air dah-lum) |
| Shallow | = Dangkal | (Dun-kahl) |
| Channel | = Saluran | (Sahl-oo-rahn) |
| Harbour | = Pelabuhan | (P'Lah-boo-hahn) |
| Boat/Ship | = Kapal laut | (Kup-ahl lout) |
| Outrigger | = Perahu | (Pr-au-hoo) |
| Sailing yacht | = Kapal layar | (Kup-ahl Lie-are) |
| Hire | = Sewa | (Say-wah) |
| Captain | = Kapten | (Kup-ten) |
| | | |
| North | = Utara | (Oo-tah-ra) |
| East | = Timur | (Tee-more) |
| West | = Barat | (Bah-raht) |
| South | = Selatan | (S'Lah-tahn) |
| | | |
| Small | = Kecil | (K'Chill) |
| Too small | = Terlalu kecil | (T'rr-la-loo K'Chil) |
| Big | = Besar | (B'Sarr) |
| More | = Lebih | (Leb-ee-h) |
| Bigger | = Lebih besar | (Leb-ee-h B-Sahr) |
| Most | = Paling | (Pahl-ing) |
| Biggest | = Paling besar | (Pahl-ing B'Sahr) |

Desert Point, Lombok

When hunting for waves in Indonesia, it really helps to take along photos of classic line-ups such as Grajagan and Jeffreys Bay to show fishermen and ask if there's anything like this nearby.

**Are there waves like this near here?**

Ada ombak seperti ini dekat disini?
(Ah-dah om-buck s'purr-tee in-ee d'kut d'sin-ee?)

Photos Piping, Cory Scott, Ron Gorringe

# CREATE YOUR OWN
# PRACTICAL LEARNING EXERCISES

Now that you have skimmed through the book, it is time to knuckle down and start to learn some of the language.

Copy words from the book that you feel you will be using. The simple act of writing the words (rather than just reading them) will imprint them on your memory much better. Just a few words to start with, so it is easier to remember. Perhaps select groups of related words and their opposites (eg. Big and Small, Young and Old, Hot and Cold etc.)

Use **The Power Of Visualisation** to imagine yourself having happy conversations with Indonesian people. Spend ten minutes with your eyes closed letting your imagination conjure up pictures of you on some remote beach talking to a local Indonesian fisherman.

Write down the kinds of conversations you hope to be having, so you will be prepared to make the most of every opportunity. Write them in English first, then translate them into Indonesian, looking up new words in your kamus. Record your conversation pieces so you can listen back to check up on your pronunciation which is very important.

Your final step is to find a personal teacher for fine tuning. You're already well on the way to speaking Indonesian like a local! Better still, just Go to Indonesia Now - there are over 250 million excellent teachers waiting to help you!

**Congratulations and good luck!**

**SELAMAT dan SEMOGA SUKSES!**

More discoveries await you in The Spice Islands, **Pacific** Indonesia

Photo: JS Callahan / tropicalpix

*kamandalu*
Resort & Spa

# hotels, restaurants
# health & travel tips

The Legian. Photo: Courtesy www.ghmhotels.com

# HOTELS & LOSMEN

Indonesia has some of the most exotic hotels and villas in the world, at prices far less than you would pay for similar hotels in Hawaii or Tahiti. You often get 5 star luxury for a 3 star price. For surfers on a tight budget, there are many $10 to $30 **Losmen**, which translates as "home-stay", often fairly close to the surf. Most started out as private homes until the family built a few spare rooms to rent out. You usually get your own fan-cooled room with private cold water bathroom. Kuta Beach in Bali has over 100 losmen from around $15 to $50 a night.

If you're only staying a week or two, check the major surf travel agents on **Page 17** for a package deal. But for a long-term low-budget trip, here are some good cheap places to start, plus some up-market hotels we recommend for families or romantic couples who want to relax in a bit of luxury:

**KUTA REEF - South Kuta Beach:**
Ultimate beachfront luxury **Discovery Kartika Plaza** from $90

**KUTA BEACH - Poppies Lane 1:**
Over 20 losmen along this lane from $15. **Poppies Cottages 1** luxurious bungalows with air-conditioning, swimming pool and A-Class restaurant, around $70, ph 751 059. **Kuta Puri** is just a minute's walk to the beach, from $35 double, ph 752 585. **Fat Yogis** is great value with a good cafe Ph 759451. **Kedin's Inn** is one of the very cheapest, around $15.

**KUTA BEACH - Poppies Lane 2, Halfway Kuta Beach:**
In the busy heart of Kuta, with over 50 great value losmen and cafes, buzzing with beautiful young backpackers from all around the world. **Poppies Cottages 2** has good value air-conditioned cottages only 100 metres from the beach, around $40, Ph 751 059. **Palm Gardens** (ph 752 198), Peter Neely's home for many years, is one of the cheapest from $15. **Cempaka** has great value traditional Balinese family hospitality from $10. Ph 754 744 <mangku66@hotmail.com>. More cheap losmen are up **Benesari Lane**, opposite **Barong Hotel**. Check **Meka Jaya**, **Kuta Suci**, Bali Dwipa, Bendesa and Beneyasa, all $15-$30.

**LEGIAN BEACH:**
Less hectic than Kuta the further north towards Seminyak. We often stay on Jalan Padma Utara, close to the best beach breaks in Bali. **Puri Raja Hotel** is right on the beach from $95. Next door is **Melasti** from $60, **Niksoma** from $235. One street off the beach: **Royal Tunjung Villas** from www.baliforfamilies.com. From $35-$50 try **Adika Sari, Sinar Indah, Three Brothers.**

**SEMINYAK, PADANG-PADANG & BALANGAN:**
Kima Surf Camps – www.kimasurf.com,£30-£40
Puri Dana Villa - 5-Star Seminyak: www.puridana.com
Aloha Bali Private Villa - www.bali-surfing.com, from $65

**BINGIN: Suara Ombak:** Five charming oceanview cottages set in a rainforest garden, unrivaled cuisine **www.wavevoice.com**

**BALIAN:** GajahMinaResort.com - Luxury 100m to surf, $70
Villa Tranquil - www.theperfectwave.com.au, $50

**ULUWATU:**
Blue Point Bay Villas - $180 to $800, Ph +62 361 769 888
UluwatuSurfVillas.com - 5 surf view Villas sleep 6 from $300
Puri Uluwatu Villas - 150m to surf, from $100. Ph 744 2552.

**EAST BALI: Keramas Surf Lodge** - www.nomadsurfers.com

**NUSA LEMBONGAN:**
Day trips & Villas: **World Surfaris** - www.worldsurfaris.com
**SUrF TRaVeL ONLiNe** - www.surftravelonline.com
**The Perfect Wave** - www.theperfectwave.com.au
**Lembongan Beach Villas** - www.lembonganbeachvillas.com

**LOMBOK:**
**Kuta Beach**: Quiet stretch of beachfront losmen, $15 to $30
Anda Cottages, Sekar Kuning, Segara Anak, Mata Hari
Guided surf trips: **World Surfaris** - www.worldsurfaris.com
New **Aman Gati** Hotel at Bangko-Bangko, near Desert Point

**SUMBAWA:**
**Nomad Tropical Resort** Sumbawa www.nomadsurfers.com
**Aman Gati**, Lakey Peak $50, www.theperfectwave.com.au

**ROTE:**
**Nemberala**: Malole, on the beach - www.rotesurfhouse.com

**SUMBA:**
**Nihiwatu**: Exclusively for guests at the 5-star eco-resort $330
**East-Sumba**: From US$35 per day, Fax Dave: 62 387 61333
**Tarimbang**: Cheap losmen from **surftravelonline.com**

**NIAS:**
**Boraspati Nias Tours**, Medan. Tom: www.boraspati.com
**Puri Asu VIP Villa**, Hinako Islands, $250, www.vipasu.com

**SOUTH SUMATRA Mainland:**
**Ujung Bocor**: Ombak Indah losmen - www.freelinesurf.com.au

**MENTAWAI Islands:**
**Wave Park Resort** - www.wavepark.com Ph +628126635551
**Aura Surf Resort** - www.aurasurfresort.com 6281376072949
**Kandui Villas** - www.kanduivillas.com +62 812 66 40941
**Togat Nusa Retreat** - www.togatnusaretreat.com 081267287537
**Kima Surf Camp** – www.kimasurf.com 62 361 736 737
**Aloita Resort & Spa** - www.aloitaresort.com 62 759 320 388
**Macaronis Resort** - www.macaronisresort.com 6281374429357
**Simeulue Retreat** North Sumatra - www.freelinesurf.com.au
**Siloinak Resort** North Sumatra - www.surftravelonline.com

**WEST JAVA:**
Cimaja Point: **Pondok Kencana** Resort overlooks 2 rights
Genteng/Turtles/Mama's: **Batu Besar** - www.freelinesurf.com.au
Batu Karas: **JavaCove** Hotel - www.javacovebeachhotel.com

**G-LAND, EAST JAVA :**
**Joyo's Jungle**: www.g-land.com - www.worldsurfaris.com
**Bobby's**: www.grajagan.com - www.theperfectwave.com.au

# RECOMMENDED HOTELS

## PURI RAJA

One of our favourite hotels in Bali, mainly because it's right on the beach at Legian, with the best beachbreaks straight out the front. Not as expensive as nearby beachfront hotels, even though it had a major refurbishment in 2006. Very casual and friendly. Two swimming pools and a restaurant overlooking the beach. A great place to relax all day, ideal for families or couples.
**Phone: 754 828 www.puriraja.com**

## POPPIES COTTAGES

One of Bali's first up-market boutique hotels back in the mid seventies. They still have a loyal clientele who come back year after year. Each thatched-roof cottage is separate from the next, set amid beautiful tropical gardens. Recently renovated, each cottage has air conditioning and hot water bathroom, with comfortable furniture on the verandah for lazing away the hours. The original Poppies Cottages are in Poppies Lane One, just 50 metres from the famous Poppies Restaurant. The second Poppies Cottages, in Poppies Lane Two, are only 100 metres from the beach. **Ph 751 059, www.poppiesbali.com**

**DISCOVERY KARTIKA PLAZA HOTEL** 5-star luxury right on Kuta Reef beach, ideal for families or romantic couples. Acres of lush tropical gardens line the beach. Sit under a swaying coconut palm watching golden sunsets dipping into the ocean. The 312 elegantly appointed rooms, suites and villas offer direct access to the beach. There are seven Food and Beverage outlets, many beachside, plus well equipped Fitness Centre, sauna room, Jacuzzi, squash courts, massage rooms, tennis courts, swimming pools and kids' club. The ultimate beachfront hotel in Kuta Beach. **www.discoverykartikaplaza.com**

When it comes to finding a great value losmen right in the heart of Kuta you can't beat **PALM GARDENS**. The price is right, from **US$**15 a night, the fan-cooled rooms are basic but clean, and you're right in the middle of Kuta's cafe and nightlife centre, Poppies Lane 2. The beachbreak waves of Halfway are just 150 metres walk away. Plus there are scores of cheap cafes, surf shops, CDs and DVDs, travel agents, internet cafes and clothing markets all around you. **Phone 752 198** to reserve a room, or just arrive by taxi any time. If they're full, try **Okie House** next door, or **Cempaka** just around the corner.

## BLUE POINT BAY VILLAS, ULUWATU

The new luxurious 5-star resort overlooking the surf right at Uluwatu. The ultimate in ocean-view comfort, popular with families and couples. Two storey villas and honeymoon suites have private plunge pools, Jacuzzi or sundeck. There's even a Wedding Chapel if the romantic setting gets you in the mood! Two superb restaurants with mediterranean, seafood and Asian cuisine, two huge swimming pools and indulgent Spa services.
**www.bluepointbayvillas.com - Ph: (62-361) 769 888**

# RESTAURANTS WE LOVE

## TUBES

The world's first surfers bar and restaurant, right in the heart of Kuta in Poppies Lane 2. Set up by Steve Palmer, Kim "Fly" Bradley and friends back in 1986 as a place for surfers to relax at night. Scene of many wild nights, video premieres, and surf contest presentations. Photo of Kelly, Riz & Rob at the 1995 Quiksilver Pro awards night at Tubes by Jenny Brymer. **Ph 753 510**

## SEASIDE Beach Restaurant & Lounge

Jalan Double Six, North Legian. Definitely the best beachfront restaurant for surfers. Right on the beach so you can watch the surf. Huge upstairs Treetop BBQ deck, big screen surf movies, live music, the cheapest cold beers, pool table, imported steaks, the freshest seafood and jumbo prawns. Incredibly cheap for such good quality food. Switched-on staff give great service with a smile - makes you want to come back again and again! **Ph 737 141** - www.seasidebali.com

## POPPIES

So good they named the street after it - Poppies Lane One, Kuta. No trip to Bali is complete without a classic night out at Poppies. Still highly popular after 30 years with their romantic garden setting and wide-ranging menu. Seafood, steaks, Indonesian. Casual sophistication and great service. If you haven't been to Poppies, you haven't been to Bali! **Ph 751 059** www.poppiesbali.com

## TJ's

Poppies Lane 1, Kuta. Excellent California-Mexican, Cajun and Mediterranean food, served in a very stylish, laid-back, comfortable setting overlooking fish ponds. We love it for their excellent fresh salads, soft tortillas, jazzy US west coast music and awesomely wicked chocolate mud cake! **Ph 751 093** www.tjsbali.com

## TEPAN NOODLE @ Discovery Kartika Plaza Resort

One of Bali's best value beachside restaurants, just off the sand to the north of Kuta Reef. Superb fresh Sushi and Sashimi, sizzling Teppanyaki hotplate, and full menu of Asian favourites, priced from just $10 to $15. Specials include grilled mahi-mahi in pandan leaf, and Japanese noodles. Open for lunch or dinner, we thoroughly recommend it for relaxing sunset cocktails. www.discoverykartikaplaza.com

# RESPECT THE LOCALS

The Indonesian local surfers will be your new best friends. If you treat them with respect you will enjoy your trip so much more. A smile is worth a thousand words in any language.

If you smile, talk quietly and give them the respect they deserve, you will develop true friendships, get cheaper bargains as a bonus, but more importantly you will gain a genuine insight into their uniquely spiritual lives and centuries old cultures. Indonesia is alive with religions like Islam, Hinduism, Buddhism, Christianity and ancient Animistic beliefs. Your spirit will come alive in Indonesia.

Many Indonesians are highly creative artists, a reflection of their spiritual and religious beliefs.  Be sure to visit an art gallery, museum, dance or musical performance. Balinese funerals and temple ceremonies are open for tourists to watch so long as you wear a sarong and waist scarf as respect for their Hindu religion. Don't climb onto temple walls to watch the ceremony as it is considered rude to place your head higher than an others.

The most exciting dance to see is the **Barong and Kris dance** where dancers enter a trance and turn long sharp kris knives on themselves. **The Fire dance** is another exciting spectacular where a tranced man rides a wooden horse through fire to exorcize demons from the village.

Although most Indonesians are quite poor by western standards, in many ways they are much richer in culture, tradition, religion, family values and the arts.

Many locals earn only **$3 a day**, with unemployment and food costs constantly rising. Many now live a hand to mouth existence, so be fair when you are trying to bargain someone down an extra 50 cents. It could mean whether they get to eat today or not.

So enjoy your bargaining sessions, but once the deal is done you can always tip them an extra dollar, or buy them a cold drink. **Be generous. Karma will reward you.**

Whenever you are dealing with the locals try to remember their situation and think from their point of view - you can make friends, have some fun and laughter, but more importantly you can **earn their respect**, which ultimately will make your surf adventure so much more rewarding.

For example, a smile and polite attitude will help you deal much better with a Policeman who pulls you over because he says you misunderstood a traffic signal, or a shopkeeper who charges you 10 cents more than a local for a bottle of water, or the over-worked $3 a day waiter in the cafe who is trying to serve you as quickly as he or she can. **Be patient.**

Top Photo: Da Hui Bali Boyz, photo Piping
Other photos Dick Hoole

*Escape into Romance*

## Imagine ...

Waking up in your own private villa looking out to the sparkling Indian Ocean. Stroll down for a surf, then relax all day at one of our spectacular ocean view pools.

Sunset cocktails poolside or on your private deck, followed by a seafood experience in our first class restaurants. Sleep to the sound of the ocean as the evening sky sparkles with ten thousand dancing stars.

**Blue Point Bay Villas & Spa** are luxury ocean front villas located in the Southern Peninsula of Bali Island, right on Uluwatu and Suluban Beach facing the Indian Ocean which is an earthly surfer's paradise

**Blue Point Bay Villas & Spa** offer you a choice of Deluxe rooms, Two Storey Villas, Split Two Storey Villas, Ocean Jacuzzi Villas, Pool Villas, Ocean Front Honeymoon Villas and Ocean Front Presidential Villas. Bali's most Romantic Wedding Chapel & Reception, The best Seafood, Mediterranean, Asian, BBQ, In room dining, Fresh & Fun Package, Swim & Fun Package, Tea Time, Day Spa, Massage, Aromatherapy and facials

**Convert your dreams into reality at Blue Point Bay Villas & Spa**
*The Right Place for Holiday, The Best Place for Wedding Ceremony and The Most Amazing Place for Surfing & Event Party*

**BLUE POINT**
*Bay Villas - Spa*

Jl.Labuansait - Uluwatu, Pecatu, Bali 80364, Indonesia.
Telp: (62-361) 769 888, 3009729 ~ 31 (Hunting), Fax: (62-361) 769 889 , 3009728
E-mail : info@bluepointbayvillas.com  Website: http://www.bluepointbayvillas.com

*B*est
Beachfront
Location in
Kuta

● *Rooms & Suites* ● *Villas* ● *Restaurant & Bar* ● *Fitness Center* ● *Kids Club*
● *Swimming Pool* ● *Sauna* ● *Jacuzzi* ● *Tennis Courts* ● *Squash Courts* ● *Massage Rooms*
● *Business Center* ● *Wi-Fi Internet Access* ● *Meeting Rooms*
● *Discovery Shopping Mall*

**DISCOVERY**
KARTIKA PLAZA HOTEL
BALI

# Bali Barrel
## SURF SHOP

Ketut Menda
Padang-Padang

Legian Street Kuta - Bali
Ph (0361) 767238, 767240  Fax (0361) 767239
Email: bali_barrel1@yahoo.co.id

# STAND UP PADDLE (SUP) & KITE SURFING IN BALI

Both **Kite Surfing** and **Stand Up Paddle Surfing** (SUP) have really taken off in Bali recently. The best conditions for both sports are during the dry season from **April to October** each year.

Balinese kids have always flown their little home-made kites in the consistent south-east trade winds of June, July and August. The best flat-water **kite** cruising spots are inside the protected east coast coral reef lagoons of Sanur, Turtle Island, Benoa and Nusa Dua. The west coast only has one protected coral lagoon at Kuta Reef, but winds are less favourable than further up the coast where only experienced kite surfers should venture due to bigger waves, stronger currents and lots of rocks. Canggu and Balian are the best areas for expert kite surfers.

### Best Beginner Flat Water Kite beaches:
Protected inside reefs for smooth flat-water cruising. Waves on the outside reefs will vary from small to huge:
Sanur - Kite Beach (Mertasari) - **www.bali-kitesurfing.org**
Nusa Dua - Geger, Sri Lanka, Benoa
Kuta Reef - safe, but often too protected from winds

### Best Expert Kite Surfing beaches:
Canggu - Very crowded with surfers, so best with onshores
Balian - Over ten kilometres of empty surf beaches
From Seminyak to Canggu - less crowded beach breaks
Nusa Dua - end section near "two islands" is less crowded

**KITE HIRE & LESSONS** Sanur: www.bali-kitesurfing.org
Ph Jankie: Mobile: +62 8133 823 5082;
Kite Shop 50m from Sanur Beach Hotel: Ph 0361 – 284 260

### Best Beginner SUP beaches: East Coast, mostly:
Oka Point, Turtle Island - Remote uncrowded right hander, needs big swell, the bigger the better! Very long paddle to break.
Baby Reef - best SUP beginner wave in Bali when small. Local SUP rentals & lessons from **www.bali-standuppaddle.org**
Blue Reef (Light house) - Great intermediate SUP waves
Hyatt Reef - great wave but often too crowded and windy.
Tanjung Left & Right - good on mid to high tide 3 to 4 feet.
Canggu area - Tugu and Berawa on small swells high tide

### Best Expert SUP beaches: West coast, mostly:
Kuta's reef breaks are usually too crowded with surfboard riders. Kudeta beachbreak - best on low tide with medium swell. Canggu area - Tugu and Old Man outside reefs are good but can be crowded with surf schools and less advanced surfers. Local SUP rentals & lessons at Tugu and Kuta: **www.supbali.com**
Balian - good choice of less crowded rolling waves.
Medewi - good pointbreak, but often too crowded.
Puri Dajuma - uncrowded reefs near Medewi. supbali.com
Uluwatu area - most breaks are too crowded and hollow
Jimbaran - good outside reefs on big swells
Nusa Dua - end section near "two islands" is less crowded.

**KUTA BEACH** - SUP HIRE & LESSONS - **SUP BALI**
Hire & lessons at Kuta, Tugu & all over Bali. Ph Shop: 737 056
Ph Pete: Mobile: +62 818 348 824 - www.supbali.com

**SANUR** - SUP HIRE & LESSONS - **BALI KITE & SUP SURF**
Ph Jankie: Mobile: +62 8133 823 5082; Shop 50m from Sanur Beach Hotel: 0361 – 284 260 - www.bali-standuppaddle.org

Peter Cox - www.supbali.com
Photo by Brad Masters

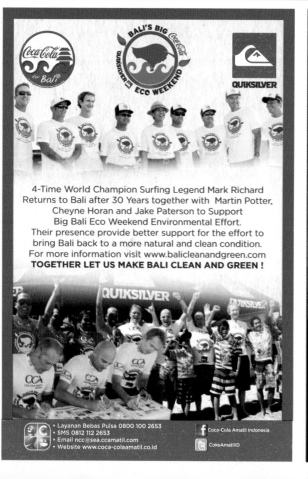

# TRANSPORT

Indonesia's roads can lead to adventure and good times, but they can also lead to an abrupt accidental end to your holiday. The roads can be extremely crowded, pot-holed and dangerous. So be careful at all times.

You'll be sharing the narrow roads with lots of traffic - trucks, buses, jeeps, minibuses, cars, motorbikes, pushbikes, soup carts, pedestrians, horses, dogs, pigs, goats, ducks and chickens. Remember, there are over **250 Million** Indonesians crammed into only 1.8 Million square kilometres, a relatively small area just a bit smaller than Mexico, or the combined size of Australian states Victoria and Queensland.

The traffic buzzes along at warp-speed, with everyone seemingly hellbent upon overtaking everyone else constantly, often two or three abreast with horns blaring. Motorbikes with a family of 5 on board will nonchalantly zoom in from side streets and blind alleys without so much as even glancing, completely oblivious of the dangerous oncoming traffic who are just expected to **give way to anything in front.**

It's not very relaxing to be driving amidst all this chaos, but just remember to keep one foot hard down on the accelerator, the other ready on the brake, and your hand on the horn. Some "rules" include constantly check your rearview mirror for overtaking trucks, and **sound your horn** whenever you approach another vehicle or person just to let them know you are there. This is considered very polite behaviour on Indonesian roads.

Remember to drive on the **left** side of the road, and beware of locals who regularly go the wrong way down "one-way" streets - **look both ways before entering any street**. The same goes for when you're out walking. Expect the unexpected.

Hazard lights flashing as a car approaches an intersection seems to mean "I'm coming through no matter what". Right flashing indicator seems to mean "I'm passing no matter what, so oncoming traffic had better pull over off my road!"

Motorbikes should expect no respect whatsoever from approaching cars who will overtake even if it means forcing you off the fringe of the road into a ditch. **Expect this to happen to you every day**. The safest rule is to give way to anything in front of you, and be very well insured.

If you intend riding a motorbike regularly bring a full-face crash helmet from home. Although when you rent a bike in Indonesia you get a compulsory helmet included, they are often just lightweight construction-style hats, with no face protection.
**Gath surf helmets** are much safer than most Indonesian helmets, and look pretty cool in or out of the water.

For many reasons, it is much better to **hire a car with a driver included**. Often it is only five dollars more, and you will be free to relax and enjoy the view while the driver's local knowledge gets you to the surf with a minimum of fuss. It can be more fun travelling with a local who will know where the locals eat, unusual sights and maybe even introduce you to his family. He can guard your belongings while you enjoy a long relaxing surf session, and you can enjoy a cold beer on the drive home.

**Taxis** are a cheap and convenient way to get around Kuta for only a dollar or two each trip. Taxi drivers might suggest a set price for your trip, but it's always cheaper to tell them to turn on the meter. They may say it is broken, or hide it with a rag. If they refuse to turn on the meter just get out. Be careful of taxis who offer you women, gambling or drugs - all are illegal. It could be a scam to rob you. Just smile and say "no thanks".

Photo by Peter Neely. Flat tyre 1975

# HEALTH

Staying healthy in Indonesia isn't always easy. Here are a few general tips, but before you go check the recommended vaccinations at the Travellers Medical & Vaccination Centre (TMVC) website **www.traveldoctor.com.au**

## water

Never, ever, drink tap water. It must be boiled or purified first. Bottled drinking water is available in most towns. You should even brush your teeth with **bottled water**. Because it's so hot, you'll perspire all day and all night, so you need to be constantly aware of preventing dehydration. Don't wait till you feel thirsty, because thirst is a sign damage has already been done. Everywhere you go, always carry a bottle of water to sip continually. Drink up especially before and after surfing. Do not swim in fresh water rivers as they may carry intestinal worms or bacteria quite similar to cholera. If you fall into a creek, don't swallow.

## accidents

The biggest danger in Indonesia is the traffic. Of the 250,000 Australians who visit Indonesia each year, around 100 end up in hospital, mostly because of motorbike accidents. If you have an accident, call Bali International Medical Centre **(BIMC phone 761 263)** in Kuta which has excellent modern medical facilities. If you need to go to hospital, don't freak out, you just need to remember to be well insured and pay in advance to get the best possible private patient treatment. Whatever you do, don't stay in the crowded public ward trying to save money. That's inviting disaster!

## food

Most tourist area restaurants serve good healthy food. However, in remote areas just remember "**boil it, cook it, peel it or forget it!**" Avoid salads as raw vegetables might be washed in unboiled water. Avoid meat from roadside foodcarts. Avoid food left out in unrefrigerated display cases (even pizza). Don't chance raw fish or raw eggs. Most people get "Bali Belly" because they forget to wash their hands before eating, drink too many fruit juices, eat too much chilli, or don't drink enough water. Wash your hands often, and always before eating.

## vaccinations

We recommend you get an online Travel Health Report from **www.traveldoctor.com.au** for the latest recommended vaccinations, but as a minimum get shots for Tetanus, Hepatitis, Typhoid, Polio. Some animals in Indonesia carry the deadly rabies disease, so keep away from monkeys and especially from mangey dogs. If bitten, don't panic, just wash in soap and water and then see a doctor for a rabies test. There is no cure for AIDS, so always use a condom. Bring plenty from home as the local ones tend to break.

## the ten commandments of hospital survival

1. Get comprehensive **Medical & Travel Insurance** before you go. It is essential you follow their claim instructions.
2. For minor accidents, take a basic First Aid Kit - see **www.indosurf.com.au/kits.html**
3. For serious accident treatment, if possible fly home or to Singapore. Your Insurance should pay for everything.
4. If imperative to operate in Indonesia - don't worry! Contact **BIMC** first for expert advice. **Phone Kuta 761 263**
5. Offer to pay in advance for a private, air-conditioned room in the hospital. The more you pay, the better.
6. Offer to pay in advance for all painkillers, antibiotics and surgical equipment.
7. Offer to pay in advance for a Private Doctor to visit you at least once a day.
8. Always travel with US$100 cash on you ready for emergencies. Money talks.
9. Ask friends or pay hospital staff to bring you fresh food and bottled water each day. It's not part of the service.
10. Accept the fact that Indo hospitals won't be as modern or efficient as back home, so don't get angry or unrealistic. The local doctors and nurses will do their very best for you, so be appreciative and thankful to them for best results.

## malaria

Malaria is a big problem in Indonesia. Bali's luxury beach resort areas are regularly sprayed and therefore 99% safe, but most other islands are not. Drug resistant strains of malaria can spread fast, so for the latest update on the right malaria pills for the islands you are visiting, contact The Travel Doctor for a Travel Health Report. You'll receive the latest information about all the vaccinations you need, the right malaria tablets and invaluable travel health advice. Then go to the TMVC centre nearest you, or see your doctor with their recommendations. Remember, surfers have died in Indonesia because they took the wrong pills. Malaria mosquitoes are very small - they make no buzzing noise, so you don't hear them coming. Their bite is lethal yet totally painless, so you don't know you've been bitten. You won't hear it, or feel it, until it's too late. So always use repellent and cover up to be safe.

Mosquitoes also carry **Japanese Encephalitis** and **Dengue Fever** which have no vaccine, so it is vital you avoid being bitten. Malaria mosquitoes bite at night, dengue fever mosquitoes bite in the daytime, so you need to use a maximum **DEET** repellent day and night. At night it is best to sleep under a bed net (or in air conditioning), reapply repellent and cover up with long sleeves and long pants from sunset to sunrise. It's better to be hot, sweaty, alive (and surfing) rather than cool, shirtless and dead.

# AIRPORT SURVIVAL

## arrival in indonesia

On board the plane you fill out a two-part Immigration Card with your Passport details and intended Hotel. Tourists from Australia, USA, UK, NZ and most surfing countries get a **30 Day Visa On Arrival** for US$25. The Visa can now be extended an extra 30 days, but requires 2 trips to Immigration wasting valuable holiday hours - it's much easier to get a **60 Day Single Entry Tourist Visa** in advance from the Indonesian Embassy in your home country. The heat and humidity will probably knock you around, so try to change into light weight clothing on the plane before you get off. Immigration will need to see your Passport and Airline Ticket out of the country, or proof of enough money to pay for your stay and flight out (US$1,000 minimum). Your Passport must be valid for 6 months after your trip ends. Store your Immigration Card safely as you must show this on leaving. Don't have too many alcoholic drinks on the plane - if you arrive drunk you will be kicked out onto the next plane back home.

## baggage claim

Pay a Porter to carry your bags for you. You'll get through the Customs and Baggage Check much quicker. It will only cost you a few Dollars. Tip at least Rp 5,000 per bag (around 50 cents). If you don't have Indonesian money yet, no worries, Porters are usually happy to accept $1 or $2 coins in your currency. They will probably ask for more, but just smile and say "This is enough sir". Your first bargaining experience!

The Customs Officer will probably look at your bags and ask "Anything to declare?" Reply with a smile "No, nothing sir." He'll quickly check your bags anyway. If he asks "How many surfboards?" reply with a smile "Only one sir." Any more than 3 boards and they will try to charge you "surfboard import tax". The tax is just a scam, no receipt will be issued, and the amount is highly negotiable. But you can't get out of paying something.

Try to pack all your boards into one bag. If you get caught with more than 3 boards, be sure to have placed $20 inside your Passport. Hand it over to the Customs officer who will most likely go into a small room for a moment and then return the Passport to you (without the cash of course) and let you through with a discreet smile. This is the "Indonesian way" and we've all just got to cop it. Remain calm and courteous. Some guys who complained loudly have been stung for hundreds of dollars.

## airport transport

Most hotels offer free pick up at the airport and transfer to your hotel. Advise them in advance that you will be bringing surfboards (especially 9 foot longboards). Their driver will be waiting outside the Arrivals hall with either the Hotel name printed on a board, or your name (mis-spelt) on a piece of scrap paper. Offer to buy the driver a cold drink, start making friends. The fun part of your adventure starts now! Revel in the warmth and humidity. P.S. That smell is clove cigarettes!

Taxis are available if you don't have a hotel transfer arranged. In Bali there is a fixed price Taxi Counter just outside the Arrivals Hall. You need to pay in Rupiah, so get some first from the Money Changer inside. The exchange rate is the worst in Bali, so we suggest you cash no more than $100. A taxi from the airport to Kuta or Legian costs around $20. Losmen rooms cost around $25, a meal costs around $15, so $100 in Indo currency should easily get you through to the next day.

## hotel check in

The Receptionist will need to see your Passport and Ticket. Never give your Passport to anyone to keep. If they need to show it to the Police to register you for example, suggest they take a photocopy. Immediately deposit all your valuables in the **Hotel Security Box**, taking a note with you of what is in the box. I suggest you relax around the hotel the first few hours, rather than charging out to the night spots or searching for waves – you may never find your way back to the hotel. Just laze around the pool, eat and drink at the hotel or close by while you get your bearings. Try to meet other tourists staying at the hotel to ask about good places to eat nearby and where the surf's been happening – they'll probably have hundreds of hair raising stories that will help you avoid the pitfalls experienced by most new arrivals. Don't buy any souvenirs in the first few days. Learn how to bargain first.

## leaving indonesia

Remember to keep **Rp 150,000** for your **Airport International Departure Tax**, plus at least Rp 200,000 for a **Taxi** to the airport and a last drink or two while you wait to fly home. Any left over Rupiah can be given as a tip to your room boy, taxi driver, or deposited in Red Cross donation tins inside the airport.

Ancient Balinese sanskrit writing saying "Matur Suksema" (Mah-tour sook-sah-moor) which means "Thank You"

# MONEY

Indonesia's monetary unit is the RUPIAH (Roo-pee-ah) symbolised as "Rp" Like Dollars, rupiah are written "Rp 1,000" but said "1,000 Rupiah". Some tourists refer to "Rupes" when speaking English, but when speaking Indonesian you should only say "Rupiah". Recently one **Australian** Dollar was worth **Rp 9,000** but the rate fluctuates daily so only change enough for a few days. The **US** Dollar has dropped drastically in the last few years, from Rp 12,000 in 2009 to below **Rp 8,500** more recently.

| | | | | |
|---|---|---|---|---|
| Ten Australian Dollars were recently worth around | Rp | 90,000 | = | AUD$ 10.00 |
| One Thousand Rupiah was worth around 11 cents | Rp | 1,000 | = | AUD$ 0.11 |
| Ten Thousand Rupiah was worth around $1.10 | Rp | 10,000 | = | AUD$ 1.10 |
| One Hundred Thousand Rupiah was around $11.00 | Rp | 100,000 | = | AUD$ 11.00 |
| One Million Rupiah was around $110 | Rp | 1,000,000 | = | AUD$ 110.00 |

It is a good idea to always carry plenty of small change. This means carrying lots of Rp 1,000 coins or Rp 5,000 notes to pay for things such as drinks, snacks, taxis, parking. In a country where the basic wage is around **$5 a day**, it is understandable that few people have change for large notes. When exchanging money ask for Rp 5,000, Rp 10,000, Rp 20,000 or Rp 50,000 notes. Try to avoid the larger Rp 100,000 and Rp 200,000 notes if possible.

Lost or stolen travel cheques can be replaced – stolen cash can not. US Dollar travel cheques are most favoured, although all currencies can be exchanged. Bali now has many **ATM** machines that accept most international Credit and Debit Cards. Check with your bank if your card is compatable with ATMs in Bali. Some ATMs have a maximum limit of Rp 600,000 (around $70). You can get larger amounts by doing a few transactions through the ATM, or from over the counter within the Banks. ATMs are fast and convenient, but safer to use in the day time rather than waiting till late at night. Remember to take a photocopy of your Passport as ID when cashing Travellers Cheques or exchanging notes inside a bank.

We recommend you avoid all small **Money Changers** as they often have "rigged calculators" and are renowned for dishonest sleight-of-hand tricks. Even bringing your own calculator doesn't make it foolproof - you will invariably get back to your hotel to find you've somehow been short-changed "as if by magic". Don't let the staff touch your money after it is counted by you. It is best to use **Banks** or large authorized Money Changers instead, even though it may cost you a dollar or two more in Commission.

Whenever you leave your hotel, during the day or night, only carry as much money as you think you will need for that trip, plus an extra 5 x Rp 100,000 notes in case of any unforseen emergency. Never carry your Passport or other valuables.

Rp 100,000

Rp 50,000

Rp 20,000

Rp 10,000

Rp 5,000

Rp 1,000

Rp 1,000

Rp 500

Rp 100

Rp 25

# RIP OFFS + SAFETY

We could fill a whole book with the scams and rip offs we have heard about over the years. But the same could probably be said for tourists going to New York, London, Sydney, Bangkok or anywhere else in the world.

Take sensible precautions and avoid trouble spots. Don't make yourself an obvious target, for example walking home drunk after a big night out - get a taxi. When you go out, only carry enough local money that you will need for that outing, plus **5 x Rp100,000** notes or **$100** for any emergency. Don't walk around with millions of rupiah bulging in your pockets.

Indonesia has endured a major economic crisis over the last ten years, so avoiding theft should be top of your mind at all times. Always lock hotel doors and windows, both day and night, even in Bali. Never leave valuables on the beach while you surf, or in your hotel room – use the hotel security box. Keep your surfboard within sight or locked inside your car, not on top.

Don't wear expensive watches, jewellery or clothes. Don't discuss politics or religion. Don't get mindlessly drunk late at night. Beware of pickpocket kids pretending to sell jewellery on Bali streets - hide your money belt or bum bag under the front of your shirt. Beware bag snatchers on motorbikes, always carry bags in your hand away from the traffic.

But don't worry, **99% of Indonesians are 100% trustworthy**, but if you are unlucky enough to be confronted by a thief in a dark alley, don't try to fight, as most thieves carry knives or have a backup gang hiding nearby - just hand over your cash and chances are they'll take it and run. Always carry a $100 note for this purpose, (a local's 1 month wages), especially at night.

Don't get too paranoid, Indonesia is generally a very safe place. 99% of toursts have no problems at all. If your only problem is that you bargained a dollar or two more for a t-shirt than the guy next door, then you've hardly been ripped off.

## visas

Either get a **30 Day Visa On Arrival for US$25** or apply to your local Indonesian Embassy in advance for a **60 Day Single Entry Tourist Visa**. You can extend the 30 Day Visa but not the 60, but you can fly to Singapore for $250 return and get another 30 day visa on return the same day. Some airlines schedule departures for just after midnight, so make sure you don't stay over 30 days, otherwise a US$20/day fine must be paid at the airport.

## registration

If staying longer than 30 days register with **www.smarttraveller. gov.au** or your country's embassy in Indonesia. They may need to find you quickly in an emergency, or to get you out of the country safely. Email friends back home regularly.

## tatoos

Be careful of temporary tatoos - if they get sunburnt they will become permanent.

## illegal drugs

Not worth the risk. Nearly 200 Australians are in jail overseas, mostly for stupid mistakes related to drugs. Never buy drugs from locals, they are almost all police informers. Buy an ounce and they'll arrest you for 10 kilos and threaten you with the Death Penalty. Drug sellers have realized they can make more money by setting you up and then bribing exhorbitant amounts of money from you or your family. Don't risk it.

## magic mushrooms

Don't be fooled into thinking eating a magic mushie omlette in the back streets of Kuta is harmless fun. The psilocybin active ingredient is virtually the same as LSD, and has been responsible for many psychotic hospitalizations over the years, not to mention the flash-backs. Bali is the last place on earth you want to find yourself tripping in hospital. The effects last for 10 hours and can be terrifying. Flash backs can recur for years. It's very illegal and carries heavy penalties.

## alcohol

Don't get mindless - most bartenders will try to short change you. Indo hangovers can be hell too, because of the intense heat, humidity and dehydration. Alternate between one beer then one water. The "ugly Aussie yobbo" has a bad reputation in Bali for inconsiderate drunkenness, so have fun but remain courteous. Never accept an open drink from a stranger, it could be spiked with sedatives. Be careful with the local **Arak Attack**, a high octane clear spirit, a bit like tequila, with a kick like an angry bull. Some local "Kuta Cowboys" don't handle alcohol very well - they can get aggressively jealous if you chat up a tourist girl they failed to charm. So enjoy yourself, but stay alert and friendly towards the locals. If you see a fight brewing, get out of there - the locals may be short, but no-one wins a fight against them - they are all experts at karate.

Prostitutes are in the business of making money. There have been a few reports that "night butterflies" as they are known (kupu-kupu malam) have stolen money from drunk or sleeping clients. But the majority of "working girls" are relatively trustworthy, very few are involved in heavy drugs, but be careful in crowded night clubs - you may be cuddled by a pretty girl or boy, only to have your wallet stolen. Prostitution is illegal in Indonesia although very widespread. The authorities have been cracking down hard on it recently. Don't try to take a local girl back to your hotel room because most Receptionists are not allowed to let them in because of previous problems with theft.

Handling the local **Police** with tact: If stopped by police for a minor traffic violation, you may need to go to court in the city. To avoid this waste of time, offer to pay an on-the-spot fine. Be sure not to call this a "bribe", just say "**Can we end this here if I pay you a fine now?**" Understand that the police are "helping you out" by accepting the fine (negotiable by bargaining) so you can avoid the trip to court. Ten or twenty dollars usually does the trick, depending upon the severity of the traffic offence. Don't expect a receipt.

# F.A.Q. frequently asked questions

## How much Money do I need?
**Hotel:** Basic losmen rooms cost from around $10 to $25. With air-conditioning around $30 to $60. For beachfront with air-con is around $80 to $150. Sometimes you can negotiate a 25% to 50% discount if you stay a week or three in low season.

**Food:** $2 - $5 for breakfast, $2 - $10 for lunch, $5 - $10 - $50 for dinner & drinks. A large 750ml beer is around $5.

**Transport:** Taxis around Kuta cost $1 to $5 per trip. Day trips to Uluwatu are around $50 for a car and driver. Self-drive cars are around $45 a day. Motorbikes are $10 to $20, experienced riders only. Public transport is very cheap, but crowded and slow.

## Can I rent or buy a Surfboard in Bali?
Yes. Lots of old boards for rent on Kuta and Legian Beach for around $10 a day. Or $25 for a new SurfTech from **526 FOOT**. New and second hand boards for sale from US$150 to $600 in **Poppies Lane 2 Kuta** at shops like Indo Dreams and The Boardshop. Boardshorts cost $10 for local brands. **Rip Curl**, **Quiksilver** and **Billabong** are cheaper than back home.

## Can I learn to surf in Indonesia?
Yes, but most Indonesian reefbreaks are too dangerous. Bali is the safest place. Check **Rip Curl School of Surf** at Double Six Beach 73 5858, or **Pro Surf** at Kuta Beach 744 1466. You can try SUP with Pete at **SUP Bali** T: 737 056 - www.supbali.com

## Are there any less dangerous breaks?
Yes. Here are Bali's "easier" breaks, in ascending order of "danger". These breaks are more suited to **longboards** too:

### May to October "Dry Season":
1. **Kuta**, Halfway beachbreak. Sand bottom, soft and safe, no need for reef boots. Surfboard rentals on the beach.
2. **Legian**, Jalan Padma. A more powerful beachbreak.
3. **Berawa** beachbreaks on next beach south of Pererenan.
4. **Pererenan**. Lava rock-reef, reef boots needed at low tide.
5. **Balian**. Round river-rock bottom, safer with reef boots. Uncrowded, relaxed country feeling at Gajah Mina Resort.
6. **Medewi**. Round river-rock bottom. You need reef boots for getting in and out over the rocks. Longboard heaven.
7. **Dreamland**. Beachbreak, but coral sand so need boots.

### Easier Reefbreaks for Intermediate Surfers:
8. **Kuta Reef** & **Airport Lefts** - coral bottom, but quite deep on high to mid tide (not low). Unlikely to hit the reef here. Jekung outriggers take you out and back for around $8.

### December to March "Wet Season":
9. **Padang Galak** - the best beachbreak on the east side.
10. **Serangan Turtle Island** - the easiest reefbreak by far.
11. **Nusa Dua**. Coral reef, but quite deep on high to mid tide (not low). Safer with reef boots. Jekungs take you out to the break and back for around $10. Out-going tide easier paddle.

# BALI SURF SHOPS

**BILLABONG:** Kuta Square T: 756 296; Corner Poppies Lane 2 & Jalan Legian; Discovery Mall Jalan Kartika Plaza T: 769 584

**THE CURL:** Jalan Legian 191, T: 765 889; Discovery Mall; Jalan Pantai 198 Kuta T: 765 141; Jalan Melasti 67 Legian 753 694

**DRIFTER:** Jl Oberoi Seminyak, 8475958 www.driftersurf.com  **DIVERSE** Surfboards, 526 FOOT Sunset Rd, Seminyak 737 056

**526 FOOT** Surf Shop - 5 Sunset Road, Seminyak T: 737 056  **BALI BARREL:** Jalan Legian, Kuta. Ph Ketut Menda 767 238

**SURFER GIRL:** Jalan Legian **138**, Kuta. T: 752 693; Kuta Square T: 753 885; Bali Collection Nusa Dua T: 775 698

**SURF TECH & SUP Rental:** 526 FOOT Sunset Rd, 737 056  **SURF TECH & SUP Sales:** 526 FOOT Sunset Rd, 737 056

**QUIKSILVER BOARDRIDERS CLUBS:** Bemo Corner Kuta; Kuta Square; Jl Legian **138** T: 751 214; Discovery Mall; Seminyak

**DA HUI** Jalan Padma, Legian, Ph Made Kasim 752 602  |  **JUNGLE SURF** Kuta Beach, Ketut 'King Kong' Kasih. 750 096
**KITE & SUP:** Sanur 284 260 www.bali-standuppaddle.org  |  **THE SURF SHOP** Jl Legian, Kuta. Wayan Gantiyasa
**INDO DREAMS** off Poppies Lane 2, Kuta. Ph Budi 758 650  |  **EXTREME TOYS 3** Jl Bypass Ngurah Rai 774 Nusa Dua
**SURFER'S PARADISE** Jalan By Pass Ngurah Rai 210, on the main road to Uluwatu, Jimbaran. T: 705 385
**THE BOARDSHOP** Poppies Lane 2, Kuta. Natalie 758 506  |  **ROCKY** Surf Shop & Transport, Jl Padma Legian 756 070
**THE PIT** Fauzan, Jl Legian 64, 2nd Floor, Kuta Ph 763 357  |  **ROXY** Jalan Legian , Kuta + Kuta Square
**SUP BALI** Kuta Beach T: 737 056 - www.supbali.com  |  **COOKIE** Surfboard Repairs, Legian. Ph 081 239 89044
**www.BaliWaves.com -** Daily Kuta Reef & Uluwatu Reports  |  **www.BaliSurfReport.com -** Daily Kuta Beach Reports

**FREELINE Jakarta** Jalan Jaksa 35, Ph (021) 3190 7145  |  **SURFER GIRL Jakarta** Senayan City Mall, Ph 021 72781731
**OMBAK TUJUH** Cimaja **West Java**, Ph (62) 0266 431465  |  **SUBSTANCE** Padang **Sumatra** - www.understance.com

# INDO SURF & LINGO - CHECK LIST

OK! So you're amped up, ready to go right now eh? But there's still lots of planning to do before you can enjoy paddling out into your first surf in Indonesia. Here's a basic Checklist of some of the things you'll need to think about before you're ready to board your airplane. It's by no means a complete list, but it's a good start.

One of the best things you can take along with you on your first overseas surf trip is **A Good Attitude**. Plan to meet lots of "strangers" who will eventually become your new "best friends". Plan to be respectful and helpful to everyone you meet. Fellow travellers and locals alike. It's a tough world out there and you're going to be all alone, so go forth and be friendly with everyone you meet. And catch a few good waves along the way.

[ ] Airline Ticket, into and out of Indonesia      [ ] Passport valid for at least 6 months
[ ] International Driver's Licence from home      [ ] **Travel Insurance** from www.indosurf.com.au
* If you can't afford insurance, you can't afford to travel - Emergency airlifts cost $50,000!
[ ] Traveller's Cheques, Credit Card      [ ] $50 of Indo small currency
[ ] Budget minimum $30 a day. $40 to $60 is more comfortable. $70 to $150 is first class!
[ ] Travel Health Plan **www.traveldoctor.com.au**      [ ] Vaccination Record Book - Vaccinate for Polio, Hepatitis, Tetanus, Typhus, Diphtheria, Smallpox. Get Malaria and Dysentery information.
[ ] 3 photocopies of all Documents. Keep 1 at home, 1 in your suitcase, 1 in your boardbag.

[ ] Surfboards (with removable fins)      [ ] Wet Shirt/Rash Shirt
[ ] Board Bag (and extra bubble wrap)      [ ] Reef Boots for everywhere except Kuta beach
[ ] Wetsuit Vest (buy surfshorts in Bali)      [ ] Sunglasses
[ ] Cap (buy a broad brim hat in Bali)      [ ] Wax - tropical warm water
[ ] Legropes - take only new ones      [ ] Gath Helmet and surfing suncap
[ ] Board Repair Kit - sun curing only      [ ] Soft racks or straps for outside Bali
[ ] Beach Towel - small and light      [ ] Sunblock, waterproof 30+

[ ] First Aid Kit - Antiseptic, Antibiotic pills and powder, Aspirin or Paracetamol, Bandaids, Diarrhoea pills, scizzors, Swiss Army knife. See **www.indosurf.com.au/kits.html**
[ ] Mosquito repellant, tropical strength      [ ] Malaria pills for all travel outside Bali
[ ] Toiletries Bag - soap, toothpaste, etc      [ ] Condoms, just in case you get lucky
[ ] Recreational drugs? Don't even think about it! Death penalties are not worth the risk.

[ ] Clothing and Shoes (pack only half what you think you'll need) It's going to be very hot and sweaty!
[ ] Books, Mags, writing paper & pens      [ ] Small flashlight, new batteries
[ ] Electrical Adaptor (two round pins, 220 volt). Surge protector if taking a laptop.
[ ] Camera, data cards, new batteries      [ ] Hotel reservation the first 3 nights, so you can get over jetlag and check out the area. See the Discounts in this book and from **www.indosurf.com.au/discounts.php**

[ ] Check for Government Travel Warnings: In Australia phone 1300 555 135, or online **www.smarttraveller.gov.au** From USA check **www.usembassyjakarta.org**
[ ] Phone numbers of friends and family at Home, in case of an Emergency
[ ] Your Itinerary - leave it with your parents so they know where to send the rescue helicopter!

[ ] Bookmark these **Swell Forecast Websites**: Some of the most accurate, up to 5 days: www.surfline.com, www.facs.scripps.edu/surf/inda.html, www.stormsurf.com, www.swellwatch.com, www7300.nrlssc.navy.mil/html/swell/bali, www.fnmoc.navy.mil/PUBLIC, www.oceanweather.com, www.bouyweather.com, www.magicseaweed.com, www.baliwaves.com, www.surf-forecast.com, www.coastalwatch.com

[ ] **Free iPhone, iPod and iPad Language Apps**: available from the Apple iTunes website www.itunes.apple.com "Lingopal Indonesian Talking Phrasebook", "Indonesian Audio Flashcards" ,"Learn Indonesian Vocabulary", "World Nomads Indonesian Language Guide" is available from www.worldnomads.com for PC, or iTunes for Mac

Pack your bags the day before leaving, label them inside and out with your Home Address and your Indonesian address (or care of your Airline). **Try dragging all your bags 100 metres**, then throw out anything heavy. Two back packs is good – one large one and a smaller day-pack. Also a "bum bag" to store money, tickets, passport and other valuables. Arrive at the airport an hour earlier than required to do some duty free shopping. On the plane relax, rest, and read all you can about the Indonesian culture on the long flight over. Learn some of the key words and phrases. Don't drink too much alcohol. Drink plenty of water and walk around the plane every hour to stay loose. Have fun!

# THE RIGHT SURFBOARDS FOR INDO

Indonesia's waves are best described as fast - very fast! Rarely do the reefs get below 4 feet, so more often than not, you'll find yourself charging down-the-line overhead tubes at full-speed! Come prepared.

Your typical small wave board from home should handle the beachbreaks and easier reefs up to around 6 feet.

A semi-gun could be your most used board, taking full advantage of the frequent 6 to 10 foot days. A full-gun surfboard for the 12 foot plus days would probably only be needed a few days each month, mostly in the peak swell season from June to August. On giant days there's usually somewhere else to surf that is a bit more manageable.

Indonesian waves rarely get over 12 feet, and they are usually fairly smooth and predictable, which means you can ride finer, shorter, more sensitive boards than Hawaii.

We asked a few of Australia's most experienced shapers of Indo boards about their favourite boards for Indonesia. All these shapers can design your dream Indo quiver.

**Outer Island** - Shaper: Mitchell Rae - Length: 6'4"

www.outerislandsurfboards.com

**The Coral Reefer** - our most advanced, high performance model. New triple turbo concaves have created our fastest, most responsive board so far. The secret is our rail concaves that generate instant speed and maximum control through all manoeuvres. The bonus turned out to be superior tube riding performance. Andy Campbell swears by his on the really sucky hollow days: "The king of concaves - no Outer limits".

**Diverse** - Shaper: Feral Dave - Length: 6' 6"

www.diversesurf.com.au

A perfect length for the perfect days that are a common reality in Indonesia. We produce over 200 boards a year for Indo surfers, from junior local champs to senior world travellers. If you want the best Indo-proven boards, check our website where you can custom design the board you want, and get your hands on your best possible travel investment. **Diverse is different!**

**Bourton** - Shaper: Murray "Muzza" Bourton - **Skinny Bullet**

www.basesurfboards.com

The **Skinny Bullet Quad** creates a faster down the line, more versatile quad fin performance. A narrower nose and round tail makes it more vertical and responsive. Ideal for bigger waves too, with our exclusive Cathederal Hull's 20% paddle advantage. Inspired by ultra-modern boat designs, the Hull's concave hydrodynamic force lifts and cushions, resulting in more drive out of turns. Muzza's zippiest fish yet!

**Bourton** - Shaper: Murray "Muzza" Bourton - **Indo Gun**

www.basesurfboards.com

The **Bourton Indo Gun** - a perfect semi-gun for Indo. After surfing Indo regularly for over 30 years, this is what you need if you really want to tackle what's on offer. A concave under the chest runs into a 3mm vee through the fins and out the tail giving the board more speed and more control through deep tubes. A stronger diagonal glass job handles the powerful type of waves they are designed to excel in!

# NOMAD TROPICAL RESORT
# WEST SUMBAWA

**nomad**surfers.com
board-riding holidays since 1995

An all Inclusive family friendly small hotel. Bring your wife, husband, kids or friends! Easy left point paddling distance 200 metres from your room. 26 Rooms and 3 Family Villas

## THE SURF

**Tropical Left**, a long easy rippable left point in front of the resort. Plus **Tropical Right** on the other side of the channel with fast takeoff that slows into deep water, perfect for beginners. Our surfguides also take you to Yoyos (10 minutes), Super Suck, Big Brother, Scar Reef, Little Bingin, Donuts and other secret spots... **NO CROWDS**… yet!

**This part of Sumbawa gets good surf 12 months a year!** June to August is biggest, perfect for Super Suck and Scar Reef, offshore winds all day. Sep-Nov and March-May can be the best at our frontyard Tropical Left and Right, glassy every morning with light winds some afternoons. Christmas, Jan and Feb are insane with easy glassy conditions

## PACKAGES From $1,280 AUD A WEEK

• 7 nights Accommodation
• Flights and transport from Bali return
• Big Buffet Breakfast, Lunch and Dinners
• Daily Surf Guide and transfers to local Breaks
• Children under 12 pay only 50%
• Speed Boat: Surfing, Fishing, spearfishing, BBQ
• 1 day Golf Green Fee and Golf Club rental

## FACILITIES

3 Family Villas 2 bedroom with private Pool. Restaurant (Western Chef), Huge Swimming Pool, 9 Hole Golf Course, Gym, Private Airstrip, Childrens Playground, Veggie Garden, Aloe Vera and Dragon Fruit Plantation, SpeedBoat 40 HP (10 pax), Snorkles, Spear fishing gear, South African Surfguide, Masseuse, Baby-Sitters, Surf Instructor, New Surfboard rental (Short and Long boards), WIFI Internet, Sat TV

## TESTIMONIAL

"Nomad Tropical Resort is one of the best I've been to. Its mellow fun and you can surf all day, at the left out front YoYo's down the road and Super Suck close by. If you want a fun uncrowded surf trip, with a variety of waves, this is the place to go!"
**John John Florence** (pro surfer)

Phone: ++62 81337670152

www.nomadsurfers.com - info@nomadsurfers.com

# RECOMMENDED YACHTS & SURF CAMPS

Aloita Resort & Spa, Mentawai Islands

www.surftravelonline.com
www.freelinesurf.com.au
www.bali-surfing.com
www.nomadsurfers.com
www.g-land.com - Joyo's
www.sumatransurfariis.com
www.wavepark.com
www.mentawaiislands.co.id
www.aloitaresort.com
www.togatnusaretreat.com
www. indo-odyssey.com
www.mentawaidaze.com
www.dreamweaver-surf.com
www.cruisebali.com
www.ombaktujuh.net
www.bluepointbayvillas.com
www.poppiesbali.com
www.wavevoice.com
www.rotesurfhouse.com

www.worldsurfaris.com
www.theperfectwave.com.au
www.kimasurf.com
www.surftravel.com.au
www.grajagan.com - Bobby's
www.addictionsurfing.com
www.nusadewata.com
www.kanduivillas.com
www.aurasurfresort.com
www.surgingwaters.com
www.thenusantara.com
www.mentawaiblue.com
www.moggybali.com
www.justdreamingsurfsafaris.com
www.lembonganbeachvillas.com
www.javacovebeachhotel.com
www.discoverykartikaplaza.com
www.puridana.com
www.uluwatusurfvillas.com

Lance's Left. Photo: Sean Davey

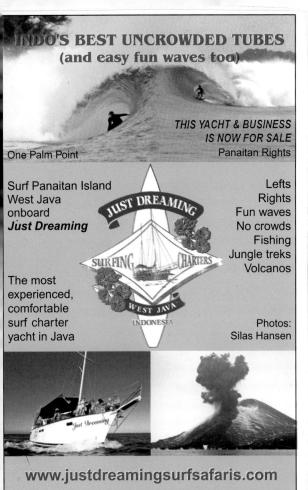
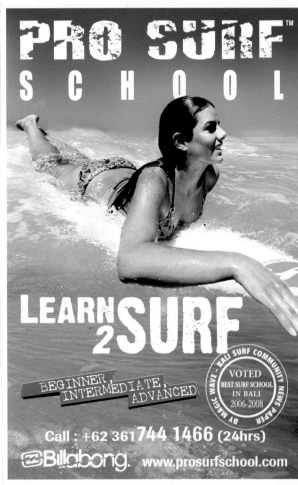

# G-Land Bobby's Surf Camp

**The Best Service**
**The Best Accomodation**
**The Best Food**
**The Best Camp**

Jl. Pantai Kuta No. 8b - Kuta - Bali - 80361 - Ph. (+62 361) 755 588 / 762 364 - bobby@grajagan.com - www.grajagan.com

# Arimbi - Mentawai Islands

**Surf the Mentawai's score Perfect Waves pull into some deep barrels and enjoy the sunny days.**
Jump onboard Arimbi and surf those uncrowded waves and perfect swell conditions that you have always dreamt of doing. The Mentawai Islands are littered with an insane amount of sick waves and secluded spots and with years of experience in the region has made Arimbi one of the best mid ranged boats in the islands.

## OVERVIEW

**We know where the waves are and when they are happening.** Arimbi is a 60ft fibreglass cruiser built in the USA in 1994 which has been customised to operate surf charters in the Mentawai Islands. 'Arimbi' has a cruising speed of 10 – 12 knots and a top speed of 18 knots. Although many of the main breaks in the area are listed below, being able to cruise around the islands means Arimbi can access every break within the Mentawai's and beyond - the only limiting factor being time and conditions.

## WAVES AT A GLANCE

**1.**
BANK VAULTS
This is a heavy, ledgy right hander with the inside bowl offering some wide pits.

**2.**
KANDUI
Kandui Left ranks as one of the fastest left-hand barrels in the world.

**3.**
MACARONIS
Commonly referred to as "Macca's" is one of the best lefts in the tropics.

**4.**
RAG'S RIGHT
Rag's Right is still working on high tide but it is no less intimidating.

**5.**
TELESCOPES
One of the world's most perfect left barrels once the swell hits 4ft or more.

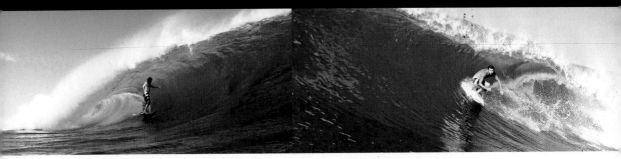

# Talk to the experts.
## surftravel.com.au
E: enquiries@surftravel.com.au P: 02 9222 8870

## FLAGSHIP STORES BALI

**SUNSET ROAD - KUTA SQUARE - MELASTI - LEGIAN
BALI COLLECTION NUSA DUA - BY PASS SANUR
POPPIES 2 - SEMINYAK - SOGO DISCOVERY MALL
NGURAH RAI DOMESTIC & INT  AIRPORT**

RIPCURL.COM

Photos thanks to John Bilderback

THE BEST WRITING
THE GREATEST PHOTOGRAPHY
AUSTRALIAN SURFING AS IT SHOULD BE

# SURFING WORLD MAGAZINE
WWW.SURFINGWORLD.COM.AU

# FLASH BACKS

**1971**, Albe Falzon and David Elfick's first trip out to Kuta Reef. The next week Albe discovered perfect surf at Uluwatu and his film "Morning of the Earth" changed surfing forever (and created millions of $ for Bali's tourism industry!)

1971 Photo thanks to Albert Falzon

**1971**, Rusty Miller and Steve Cooney, the first surfers to ever paddle out at Uluwatu. 10 Foot surf, no legropes.

1971 Photo Albert Falzon

**1973, Dick Hoole** in Singapore, on his way to Bali for the first time. Dick had just bought his first 35mm camera, so asked his friend Jack McCoy to take a few snaps. Photos created with that camera filled Tracks magazine for years.

**1975** Peter McCabe and Terry Fitzgerald, on their way to G-Land to stay in Boyum's jungle surf camp. Dick Hoole & Jack McCoy came along to create "Tubular Swells", the first film to document G-Land, Shipwrecks, and Padang Padang

# FLASH BACKS

**The first surfer in East Java?** Riding Peter Neely's surfboard in **1981** at Rajawesi, west of G-Land. This kid kept surfing for decades, until his village was wiped out by a tsunami and all his boards (donated by Fly and Gringo) were washed out to sea.

1981 Photo by Peter Neely

**1979 Nusa Lembongan.** These happy-go-lucky naked boys are probably now the respected elders of the village. Show this photo to the locals when you go to Nusa Lembongan to see if they recognise their grand fathers or uncles.

1979 Nusa Lembongan Photo by Col McLauchlan

**1974 Uluwatu.** You had to walk 3 kilometres through cactus-lined cow paddocks just to get to the beach. On the way you'd pass through this family's backyard and be greeted by happy smiling children calling out "Hello Mister".

**1975 Jalan Legian.** The road was still dirt in 1974. This was the edge of Kuta, yet only 100 metres from Bemo corner, 100 metres south of Poppies Lane 2. From here to Legian was 3 kilometres of palm trees, no shops, totally dark at night.

# about the author, peter neely

Peter Neely has been surfing Indonesia for over 35 years, since April 1975, with eight years spent full-time in Bali from 1979 to 1986, then annual trips ever since. He has spent well over 15 years of his life in Indonesia. He was a judge at the first **Om Bali Pro Surf Contest** in 1980 and won the 1995 **Bali Legends Surfing Contest** held at solid 6 foot Kuta Reef. This book was first published in 1992 and continues to be updated annually, and is widely referred to as "**The Indo Surfer's Bible**".

**Peter says:**
"I was lucky enough to surf some beautiful uncrowded waves with all the original Bali surfing pioneers back in the 1970's, guys like the late Legends Ketut 'Big Froggy' Jati, Wayan Suwenda and Wayan 'Billy' Badra; Also Gede Narmada, Wayan Sudirka, Nyoman 'Bobby' Radiasa and Ketut 'King Kong' Kasih. These first Balinese surfers were incredible to surf with, they had lots of fun in the water, always joking and laughing. You have to understand that these guys were rebels, breaking centuries of Balinese tradition, venturing into the 'evil waters'. So their joy at discovering the fun of surfing was inspiring. They became role models for the next younger generation, guys like Ketut Menda, 'Cookie', Made Kasim, Wayan Gantiyasa, and then later on Rizal Tanjung, Pepen Hendrix, Lee Wilson and dozens of other Balinese surfers who are now sponsored and travelling all over the world just to surf."

Bali, 1975                     Poppies Lane Kuta, 1975                                    Sumbawa, 1989

# indo surf & lingo
## updated every year since 1992

| 1992-1995 | 1996-1999 | 2000-2004 | 2005-2007 | 2008 - 2010 |
|---|---|---|---|---|

# www.indosurf.com.au

"Some of the most precious memories of my life are those idyllic late-70's sunset sessions at Halfway Kuta, watching the locals laugh as they surfed across the golden walls of water. It's a whole different world out there in the ocean, looking back at palm trees and volcanoes, and I feel truly blessed to have experienced those dream-like years in Bali. These days when I return each year, the warm greetings from those old friends I often see in the surf are absolutely treasured.

Even now, as the facade of Kuta has changed with the growth of tourism, completely unrecognizable from the quiet fishing village I fell in love with back in the seventies, the warmth of the people remains. Despite 35 years of change, not to mention the tragedy of terrorist bombs in what was once paradise, the Balinese spirit prevails, the Magic is still there.

I guess I've had a lifelong love affair with the waves and people of Indonesia, and my book is the result. I hope it inspires you to learn some of the language, and experience all the wonders of Indonesia for yourself."

"Selamat Jalan - may your road be blessed"     Peter Neely

Sumbawa, 1989                                                                                                    Kuta, 1975

Photos: Thanks to Dick Hoole, John S Callahan, Piping, Jon Huberman, Peter Crawford, Cory Scott, John Hepler, Shane Peel, Alan Van Gysen, Sebastian Imizcoz, Christie Carter WavePark, Surf Travel Co, Rip Curl Indo, Paul Kennedy, Stuart Horstman Freeline, Yassine Ouhilal, Mark Newsham, Jason Kenworthy, Damea Dorsey, Brian Bielmann, Albe Falzon, Brian Nevins, Emiliano Cataldi, Jason Reposar, Nathan Lawrence, Paul Gallegos, Scuzz Sumatran Surfariis, Mick Curley, Pete Cox supbali.com, Daniah, Ted Grambeau, Ron Gorringe, Jim Bristow Baliwaves, Ethan Ford, Oakley Indonesia, David Puu, Pat Koroman, Tim McKenna, Sean Davey, Andrew Shield, Pete Frieden, Gory Spain, Tim Hain, Hilton Dawe Billabong, Steve Levine, Larry Pierce, Tom Danby, Wayne McCormick, Carl Stone, Troy Sinclair, Captain Heri Sri Noa Noa, Santosha Wau, Russ Hennings, Kate Gerson, Russell Ord, Simon Hodson, Stuart Gibson, Tipi Jabrik, Troy Roennfeldt, Jenny Brymer, Per Ranheimer, Ricardo Borghi, Josh Symon, Lynden Paxton and Trevor Murphy. Map artistry by Mark Benton.

Thank you to all the people who taught me Indonesian:
The late Nyoman Rona, Tony Elliot, Wayan Mujiati Yanto, and especially my second mother Bu Badung. Terima kasih!

© Copyright & First Published 1992. Written by Peter Neely
Design by Lynne Neely, Peter Neely, Suroto
Printed in Bali by Indographs - www.indographs-printing.com

The author-publisher has attempted to check that all the information in this book is correct, however he cannot accept responsibility for any loss, injury or inconvenience sustained by any person using this book. Prices change, people move, progress happens. Please write in with updates, suggestions or photo contributions - they are always welcome. Please email <peter@indosurf.com.au>

Indo Surf & Lingo
PO Box 50 Peregian Beach, Qld 4573, Australia
Tel & Fax: (+ 61) (07) 5448 3959

Mail order copies of this book are available from our Website:

www.indosurf.com.au     ISBN 9780957724655

# FLASH BACKS

**Kim "Fly" Bradley, RIP.** One of the first surfers to live in Bali. From 1973 Fly explored all over Bali, then led some of the first surf expeditions to the outer islands. Fly helped establish The Bali Surfing Club, and was the first to shape surfboards in Bali. RIP.

1989 Fly @ Periscopes, Sumbawa. Photo: Peter Crawford

Fly's good friend Pak Manis with one of his classic mid 1970's boards. Photo: Peter Neely

141

Share a little love...
keep Bali's beaches clean.

www.gus-bali.org

OUR OCEANS
AREN'T THE
ONLY ONES
IN DANGER
MAKE A DIFFERENCE.
JOIN SURFRIDER.ORG.AU

SURFRIDER
FOUNDATION

# MORE FREE VOUCHERS!

## OVER $500 WORTH OF DISCOUNTS & FREE DRINKS
## COMPLIMENTS OF "INDO SURF & LINGO"

# MORE FREE VOUCHERS!

## OVER $500 WORTH OF DISCOUNTS & FREE DRINKS
## COMPLIMENTS OF "INDO SURF & LINGO"

144